Adventu
Phonics
Level A

- SECOND EDITION -

Written by: Florence Lindstrom

This book is dedicated
to my precious children's children
who are such a joy and blessing from the Lord.

May each student who completes these lessons
seek to glorify God in their preparation
to be our country's future leaders.

The fear of the Lord is the beginning of knowledge:
but fools despise wisdom and instruction.
My Son, hear the instruction of thy father,
and forsake not the law of thy mother:
for they shall be an ornament of grace unto thy head,
and chains about thy neck.
Proverbs 1:7-9

Ad maiorem

Dei gloriam

• A PUBLICATION OF •

Christian Liberty Press

502 West Euclid Avenue,
Arlington Heights, Illinois 60004
www.christianlibertypress.com

Layout & Graphics by: Darrel A. Trulson
Cover Design by: Bob Fine

Adventures in Phonics - Level A

The fear of the Lord is the beginning of knowledge:
but fools despise wisdom and instruction.
My Son, hear the instruction of thy father,
and forsake not the law of thy mother:
for they shall be an ornament of grace unto thy head,
and chains about thy neck.
Proverbs 1:7-9

• A PUBLICATION OF •

Christian Liberty Press

502 West Euclid Avenue,
Arlington Heights, Illinois 60004
www.christianlibertypress.com

Layout & Graphics by: Darrel A. Trulson
Cover Design by: Bob Fine

Table of Contents

Adventures in Phonics - Level A

Introduction

The importance of being able to read cannot be overstated. It gives our minds access to endless knowledge -- the greatest being God's Holy Word. It is such a blessing to gain understanding through listening and speaking. How wonderful it is to also know how to read and write as thoughts and friendships are shared.

Each loving and caring teacher knows the joy of seeing a student, after many diligent hours of studying, suddenly realize he understands how to read. It is as if a light has turned on. The student knows he can do something that is most valuable to him.

The phonics lessons contained in this workbook have been successfully used in the Christian Liberty Academy day school for over ten years. In addition, the *Adventures In Phonics* program has been field tested over a period of several years with numerous home school families who have found the pages to be very helpful. Much of the material has been developed with the help of many ideas obtained over the past twenty-five years from teachers, textbooks, and other resources. This help has been greatly appreciated.

The general plan of this workbook includes the introduction of phonetic principles in a logical sequence, along with a consistent dose of drill and repetition of these concepts to insure comprehension. Students are often directed to demonstrate their comprehension of lesson material by way of written exercises. Ideally, students should be encouraged to complete most of these exercises by themselves. However, some students may become unnecessarily frustrated with the quantity of written work which appears throughout the book. Therefore, instructors should feel free to allow their students to complete some of their workbook lesson orally. Perhaps some of the written exercises can be completed orally by the student while the teacher fills in the student's answers. Instructors are encouraged to be sensitive to the individual capabilities of each of their students, especially in the area of handwriting development.

This book is only possible because of God's gracious goodness in direction and strength. His faithfulness has granted the perseverance and guidance. From the beginning to the end of our life of learning, line upon line and precept upon precept, may we always be conscious of the fact and thankful that it is God who has fearfully and wonderfully made us. May each of us show our love and gratitude to Him in constantly seeking to be lovingly obedient. He alone deserves all praise.

Florence M. Lindstrom
Arlington Heights, Illinois

Short Vowel **a** - **A**

As you learn each letter, just say the **sound** of each letter and not the name. The first vowel to learn is the letter sound of **a** as in ant. On this page the **a** sound is at the beginning of the words. After you have said each picture word three times, underline the **a**. Look at the picture card and see the three ways **a** may be printed. People usually print it as **A** or **a**. A typewriter may print it as **a**.

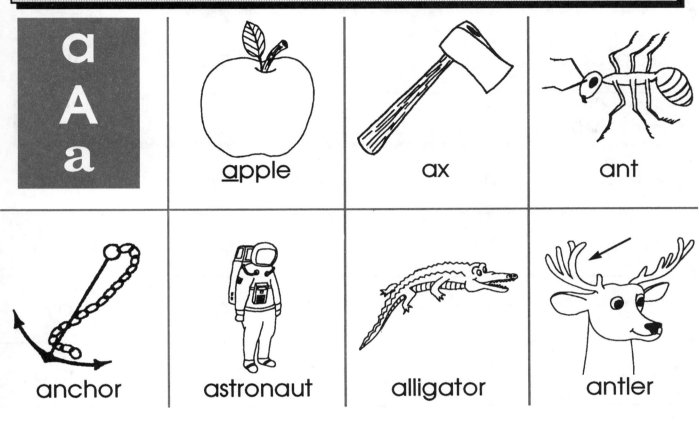

| a A a | apple | ax | ant |
| anchor | astronaut | alligator | antler |

Circle each **a** sound you see below. Say the short sound of **a** as you circle it.

a A e a a p s A

A o a a u a A a

a a A d g a n q

a m i a v b a a

Adventures in Phonics - Level A

Listen to the a sound as you say these words. Underline the beginning a.

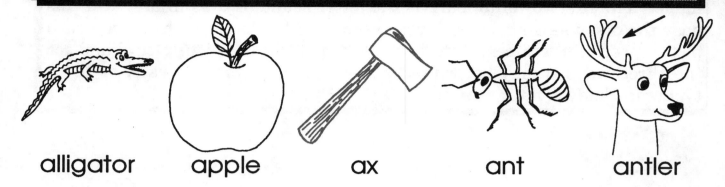

| alligator | apple | ax | ant | antler |

Many of these words begin with the a sound. Always look at the first letter. Circle only the a sound words. Listen as your teacher reads them to you.

Alice	Ann	sunny	Allen	Andy
and	after	cat	add	answer
angry	ash	ask	act	boy
accident	as	at	basket	Annie
alligator	him	ant	animal	absent
bunny	antler	acrobat	astronaut	anchor
an	axis	Andrew	admire	alligator

Say the sound of the letter as you carefully trace.

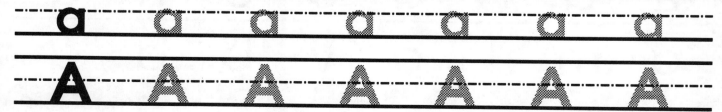

Short Vowel **a - A**

Do you remember the **a** sound as in ant? The first row has the **a** sound at the beginning of the words. Say the words and listen for the **a**. Circle the **a** sound as you say the name of the picture.

astronaut   ant   apple   ax   animals

The **a** sound is in the middle of these words. As you say the pictures, listen for the **a** sound. Underline the **a** sound. Say each picture three times.

b<u>a</u>g	cap	bat	cat	wax
fan	pan	tag	sad	man
hat	ham	map	jam	rat

- 3 -

The names of these pictures have the **a** sound in them. Carefully print **a** in each space as you say the words. Do you hear the **a** sound?

m _ n	c _ t	b _ ss	b _ t
t _ g	h _ m	h _ t	c _ n
m _ p	p _ n	f _ n	c _ p

Say the sound of the letter as you carefully trace.

a a a a a a a a

A A A A A A A A

Short Vowel e - E

The next vowel to learn is the letter sound of **e** as in elephant. Listen as you say the names of these pictures. After you have said each picture word three times, underline the first **e**.

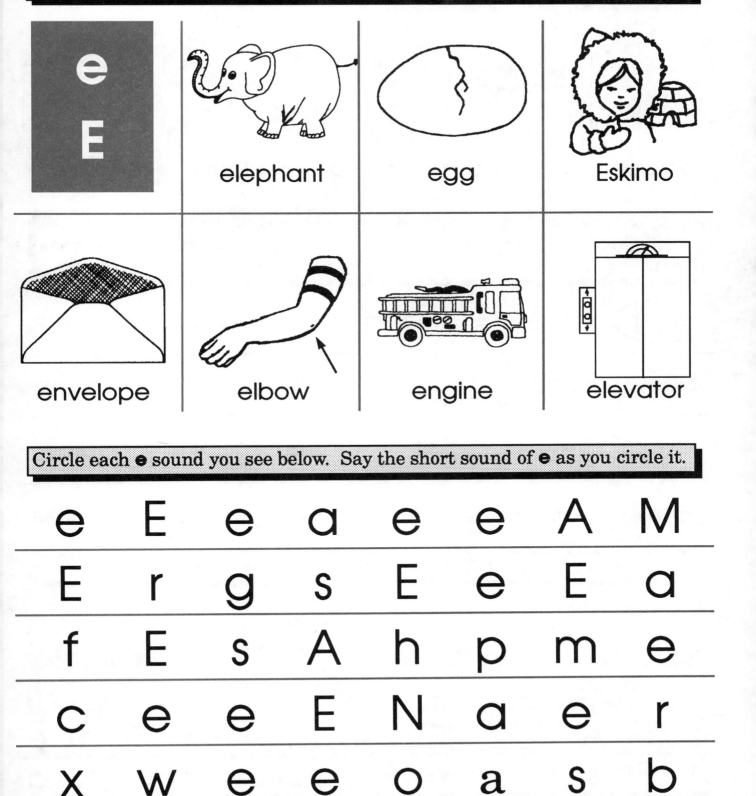

| | elephant | egg | Eskimo |
| envelope | elbow | engine | elevator |

Circle each **e** sound you see below. Say the short sound of **e** as you circle it.

e E E e a e e e A M

E r g s E E E a

f E s A h p m e

c e e e E N a e r

x w e e e o a s b

Remember to say only the **sound** of the vowels as you have heard them in **a - alligator** and **e - elephant**. Listen to the **e** sound as you say these words. Underline the beginning **e**.

elevator	engine	Eskimo	elbow	envelope

Many of these words begin with the **e** sound. Look at the first letter of each word. Circle the word if it begins with **e - E**. Listen as your teacher reads them.

(enter)	ask	Ethel	ant	engine	sleep
elbow	cat	end	Eddie	Evan	camel
Ted	every	sit	edge	ever	father
Emily	Jane	Elmer	answer	Ed	Emma

Circle each **e - E** on the left side and each **a - A** on the right side.

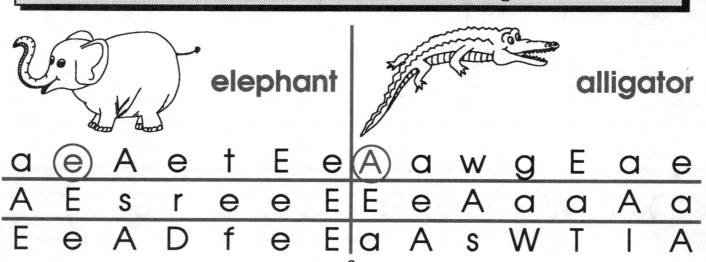

elephant   alligator

a	(e)	A	e	t	E	e	(A)	a	w	g	E	a	e
A	E	s	r	e	e	E	E	e	A	a	a	A	a
E	e	A	D	f	e	E	a	A	S	W	T	I	A

Short Vowel e - E

Think about the sound of **e** as you say these word pictures. Do you hear the **e** sound at the beginning of each word picture? Circle the **e** sound as you say the name of each picture.

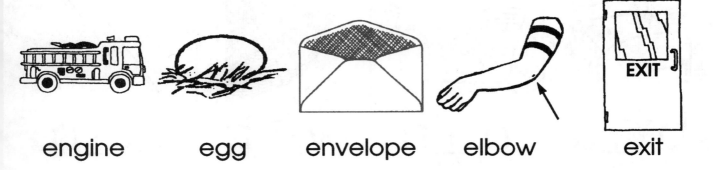

engine   egg   envelope   elbow   exit

The **e** sound is in the middle of these words. As you say the pictures, listen for the **e** sound. Underline the **e** sound. Say each picture three times.

bed   bell   ten   sled   tent

web   hen   nest   pen   steps

Say the sound of the letter as you carefully trace.

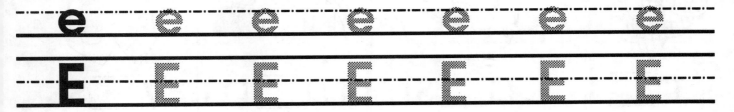

e e e e e e e

E E E E E E E

- 7 -

The names of these pictures have the e sound in them. Carefully print e in each space as you say the words. Do you hear the e sound?

b _ _ d	h _ n	w _ _ b	p _ n
d _ _ sk	g _ _ m	t _ _ n	t _ nt
l _ g	st _ _ ps	j _ t	sl _ _ d
n _ _ t	n _ _ st	m _ _ n	v _ _ st

Review of Short Vowels a - A and e - E

This lesson has words that have the short sound of **a** as in ant and **e** as in elephant. Listen carefully to see if you know which of these sounds is in each word.

a   ant

e   elephant

 n _ t	 h _ n	**10** t _ n	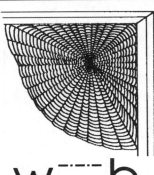 w _ b
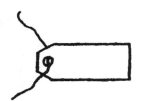 t _ g	 w _ x	 m _ p	 p _ n
 c _ p	 w _ ll	 m _ n	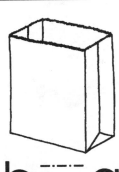 b _ g

Say the sound of the letter as you carefully trace.

A A A A a a a a E E E E e e e

Listen carefully as you say the names of these words. Which short vowel sound do you hear? Is it **a** as in ant or **e** as in elephant?

| a   ant | e   elephant |

b _ _ d

c _ _ t

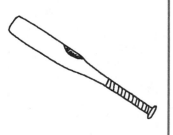

b _ _ t

p _ _ n

h _ _ t

b _ _ ss

10

t _ _ n

t _ _ nt

j _ _ t

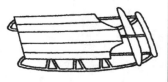

sl _ _ d

v _ _ st

s _ _ d

Say the sound of the letter as you carefully trace.

A A A A a a a a E E E E e e e

- 10 -

Short Vowel i - I

This page teaches the sound of **i** as in insects. Listen for the short sound of **i** as in insects as you say these pictures. After you have said each picture word three times, underline the beginning **i**.

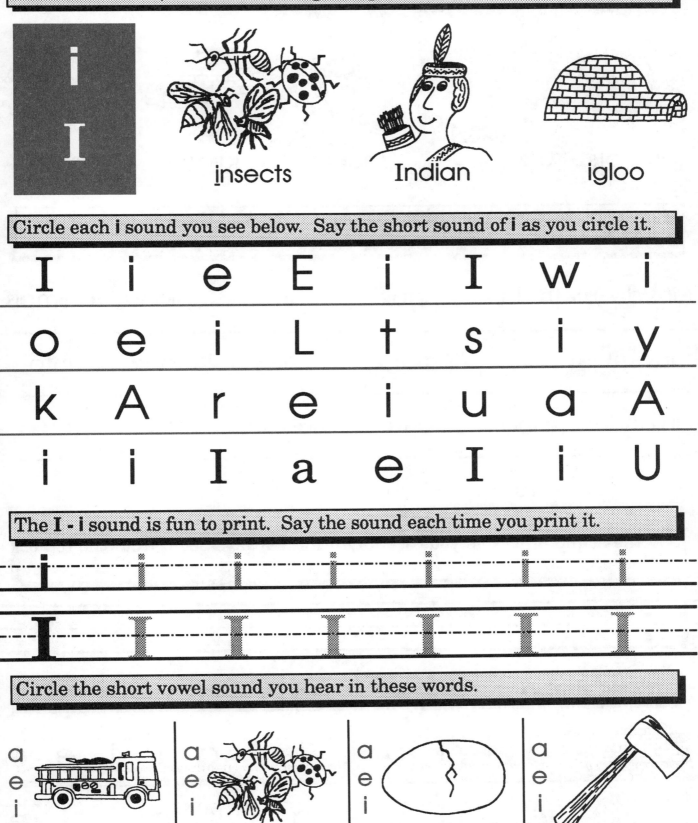

i
I

insects   Indian   igloo

Circle each **i** sound you see below. Say the short sound of **i** as you circle it.

I i e E i I w i

o e i L t s i y

k A R e i u a A

i i I a e I i U

The **I - i** sound is fun to print. Say the sound each time you print it.

i   i   i   i   i   i   i

I   I   I   I   I   I   I

Circle the short vowel sound you hear in these words.

a   a   a   a
e   e   e   e
i   i   i   i

Think again about the short vowel sound of **i** as you say the names of these pictures. The **i** sound is at the beginning of each word.

insects   ink   Indian   igloo   inside

Many of these words begin with the **i** sound. Look at the first letter of each word. Circle the word if it begins with **I - i**.

(inside)	Indian	apple	it	Indiana	animals
invite	is	image	inner	indoors	into
inland	and	after	include	Italy	India
if	under	itch	Africa	infect	in

Say the sound of **I - i** as you carefully print. Always begin from the top of the letters.

I i I i

Circle the short vowel sounds you hear at the beginning of these pictures.

d i I a E i I a I i e e

A a I E A a a A a i I e

Short Vowel i - I

| insects | igloo | ink | Indian | inside |

six	pin	hill	pig	bib
lid	fist	gift	milk	chick
fin	sit	ship	fish	clip

Adventures in Phonics - Level A

Think about the short sound of i as you carefully print it in the middle of these words.

f _ _ n   l _ _ d   m _ _ lk   g _ _ ft

s _ _ t   l _ _ ps   h _ _ ll   sh _ _ p

wh _ _ p   6   s _ _ x   f _ _ sh   m _ _ tt

Think carefully as you print the correct sound in these words.   a   e   i

c _ _ t   p _ _ n   b _ _ g   h _ _ n

Review of Short Vowels a - A, e - E and i - I

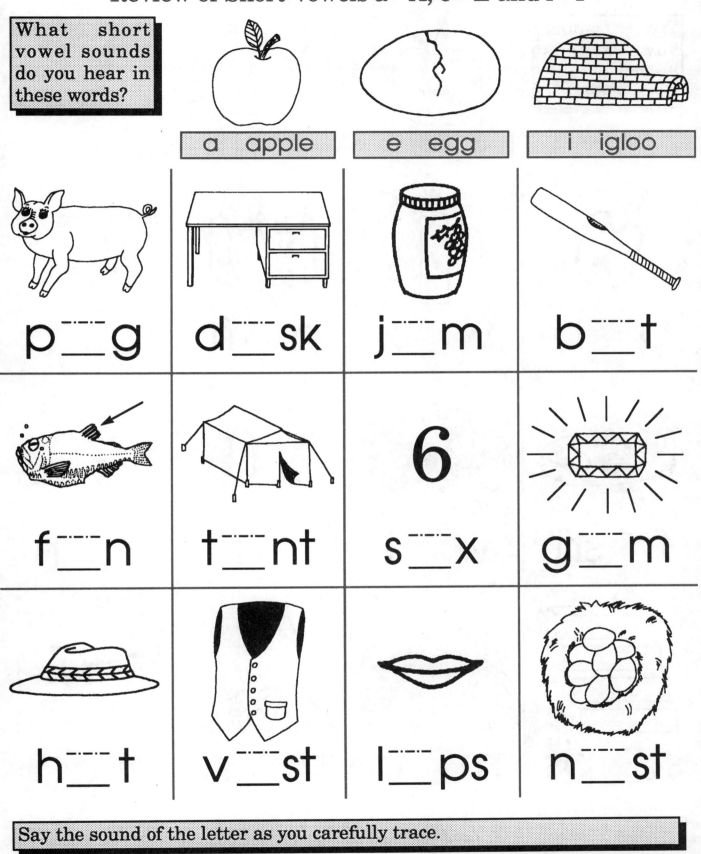

What short vowel sounds do you hear in these words?

a   apple   e   egg   i   igloo

p__g   d__sk   j__m   b__t

f__n   t__nt   s__x   g__m

h__t   v__st   l__ps   n__st

Say the sound of the letter as you carefully trace.

A a a E E E e e e I I I i i i

- 15 -

| What short vowel sounds do you hear in these words? | a apple | e egg | i ink |

b _ b | w _ x | g _ ft | m _ p

f _ sh | w _ t | t _ n | p _ n

st _ ps | m _ n | m _ n | p _ n

Say the sound of the letter as you carefully trace.

A a a E E e e e I I I i i i

Short Vowel o - O

This page teaches the sound of **o** as in otter. Listen for this sound at the beginning of the words as you say these pictures. After you have said each picture word three times, underline the beginning **o**.

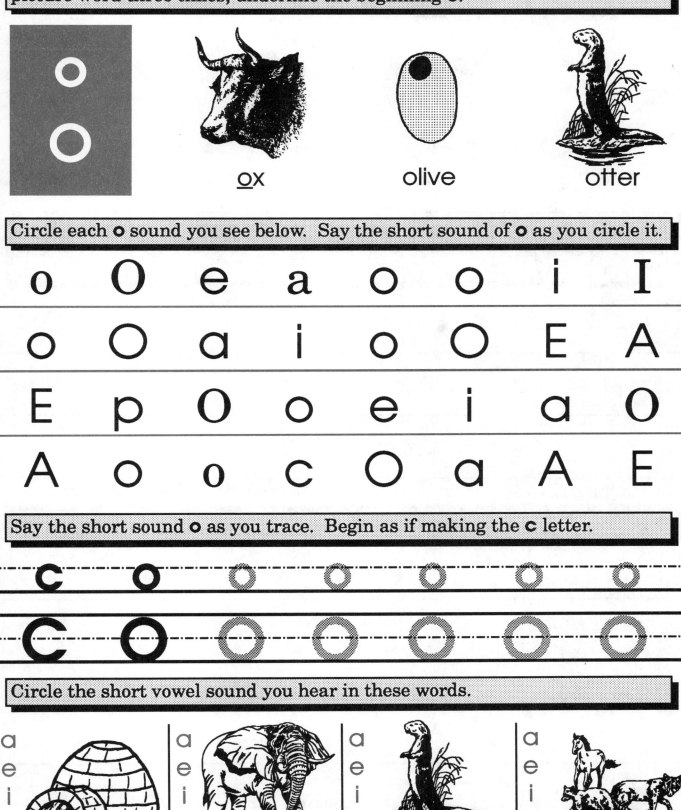

o<u>x</u>

olive

otter

Circle each **o** sound you see below. Say the short sound of **o** as you circle it.

o O e a o o i I

o O a i o O E A

E p O o e i a O

A o o c O a A E

Say the short sound **o** as you trace. Begin as if making the **c** letter.

Circle the short vowel sound you hear in these words.

a e i o

a e i o

a e i o

a e i o

Think again about the short vowel sound of **o** as you say the names of these pictures which begin with **o**. Do you hear the **o** sound? Underline the **o** after you have practiced saying the pictures.

ostrich   ox   otter   octopus

Many of these big words begin with the **o** sound. Look at the first letter of each word, and circle it if it begins with **O** or **o**. Listen for the **o** sound as your teacher reads the words to you.

(onto)	octopus	ant	oxen	Esther	object
apple	odd	oblong	otter	enter	inside
Oscar	on	Oliver	in	operate	obtain

Circle the short vowel sound you hear at the beginning of these pictures.

I e E i I i o A I a e i

e i o a E e O i e I E a

A e I a i A A o A E i A

O e I o e O a I O a e i

- 18 -

Short Vowel o - O

The **o** sound is in the middle of these words. As you say the pictures, listen for the **o** sound. Underline the **o** sound as you say each picture three times or more.

doll	top	dog	rock	sock

box	rocket	pot	rod	block

Say the short sound **o** as you trace. Begin as if making the **c** letter.

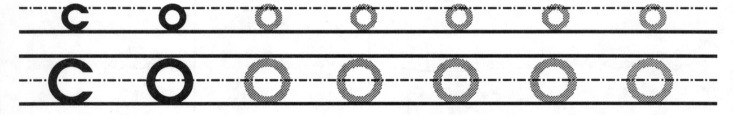

C O

C O

Circle the short vowel sound you hear at the beginning of these pictures.

a A E o a	e A A a i I	I i e i i	o d i a A
e o O A a E	E e o i E e	i n A E o	E o e i o

Do you hear the o as you say these pictures? Carefully print the o sound to make the words below.

m__p   b__x   r__ck   t__p

d__ll   c__t   r__d   s__ck

f__x   l__ck   cl__ck   h__p

Circle the short vowel sound you hear in these words.

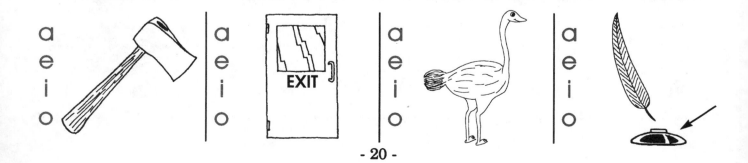

a e i o

a e i o

a e i o

a e i o

Review of Short Vowels a - A, e - E, i - I and o - O

b_ _x   h_ _m   s_ _x   h_ _n

m_ _tt   m_ _lk   p_ _n   c_ _t

h_ _p   b_ _ss   m_ _p

Need to buy:
*milk
*cereal
*coffee
*fruit
*meat

l_ _st

Say the sound of these letters as you read and trace them.

a   e   i   o   o

A   E   I   O   O

Adventures in Phonics - Level A

r __ ck	b __ ll	h __ ll	m __ p
cl __ ck	g __ ft	j __ t	g __ s
d __ ll	b __ t	r __ d	p __ g
t __ n	b __ g	n __ st	l __ ps

- 22 -

Short Vowel u - U

To help you learn the short sound of **u**, listen to the beginning sound as you say the names of the pictures three times. Underline the **u**.

u
U

<u>u</u>mbrella   umpire   up

Circle the **U - u** sound below. Say the short sound of **u** as you circle it.

U u a i e e a u

u U u u o i u o

O o U a u u U o

u u U A i i p U

Say the **U - u** sound as you print it.

Circle the short vowel sound you hear in these words.

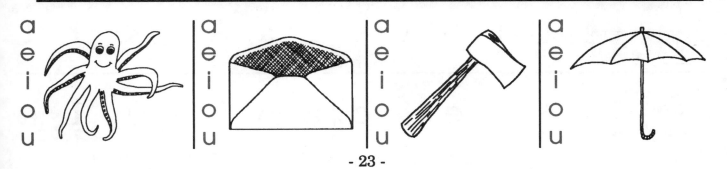

Think again about the short vowel sound of **u** as you say the names of these pictures which begin with **u**. Do you hear the **u** sound? Underline the **u** after you have practiced saying the pictures.

umbrella   under   up   umpire

Many of these words begin with the **u** sound. Always look at the first letter. Circle only the **U - u** sound words. Listen as your teacher reads them to you.

uncle	us	pirate	alligator	upon	upset
usher	answer	up	ant	umpire	unfair
ugly	until	time	stand	otter	into

Circle the letters that begin with the same sound as the pictures.

o O e I O a O e i o O a

e E i a e u E O i A e E

i i a i e I a A U e i I

A a e i o a A E e A I a

Short Vowel u - U

Listen for the **u** sound in the middle of these words. After you have said each word three times, underline the **u**.

| cup | jug | drum | duck | bug |

| club | gun | plug | gum | tub |

Say the short sound **U - u** as you trace.

u U U U U U U U

U U U U U U U

Circle the short vowel sound you hear at the beginning of these pictures.

| o o o i E | E E e o A | U i u u e | I i i e u |
| a u e o a | i a A A e E | E i u U e u | i i a u i |

- 25 -

Adventures in Phonics - Level A

Think about the short sound of **u** as you carefully print it in the middle of these words.

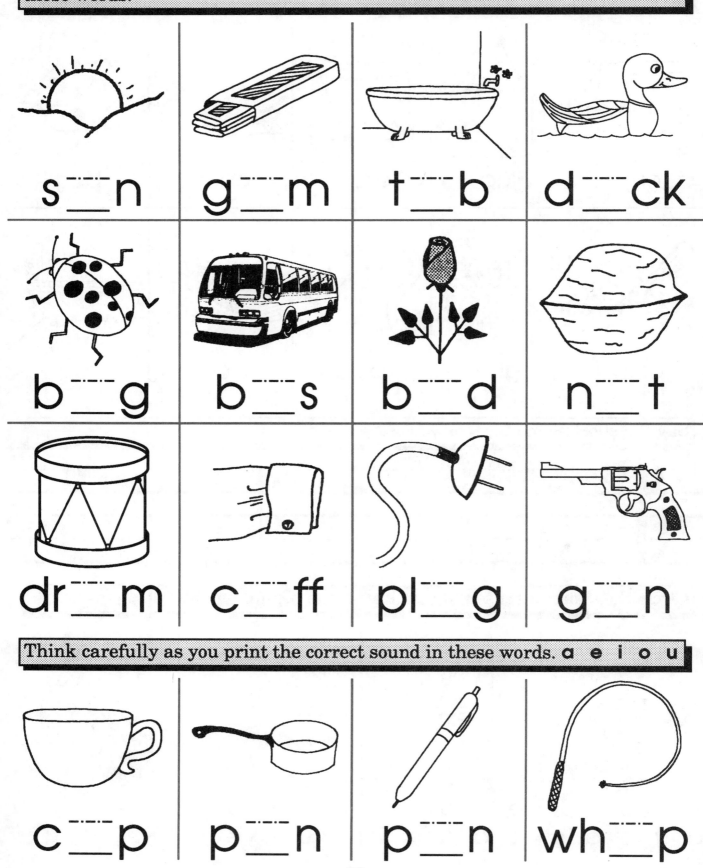

s __ n   g __ m   t __ b   d __ ck

b __ g   b __ s   b __ d   n __ t

dr __ m   c __ ff   pl __ g   g __ n

Think carefully as you print the correct sound in these words. **a e i o u**

c __ p   p __ n   p __ n   wh __ p

Review of Short Vowels a - A, e - E, i - I, o - O and u - U

j _ _ m	f _ _ n	m _ _ p	c _ _ st
d _ _ ck	t _ _ g	h _ _ n	dr _ _ m
d _ _ ll	h _ _ nd	f _ _ sh	b _ _ d
10 t _ _ n	J _ _ n	j _ _ ck	sh _ _ p

Adventures in Phonics - Level A

What short sound vowels do you hear in these words?   a e i o u

m__p	r__d	l__st	v__st
j__t	v__n	m__tt	w__ll
l__mp	s__x	g__ft	b__b
p__t	p__t	c__p	l__g

6

- 28 -

This lesson teaches the sound of the consonant **S - s** as in squirrel. Listen for that sound as you say the name of these pictures. Circle the word if it begins with **s**. Cross out the other pictures.

s / S	saw	scroll	basketball
seal	moose	soap	snail

Say the sound as you circle the **S - s** letters.

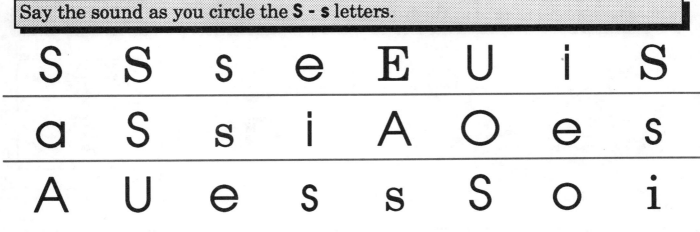

S   S   s   e   E   U   i   S

a   S   s   i   A   O   e   s

A   U   e   s   s   S   o   i

Say the **S - s** sound as you practice printing it.

s   s   s   s   s   s   s   s

S   S   S   S   S   S   S   S

Circle only the words that begin with the **S - s** sound. Listen as your teacher reads them to you.

(Savior)   silent   time   empty   engine   sandal

---

guess   Sam   so   sleepy   Tom   slow

---

sunny   man   selfish   simple   always   the

Try to say a vowel sound after you have said the **s** sound.

a	e	i	o	u
sa	se	si	so	su
Sa	Se	Si	So	Su

Circle the sound that is at the beginning of these pictures.

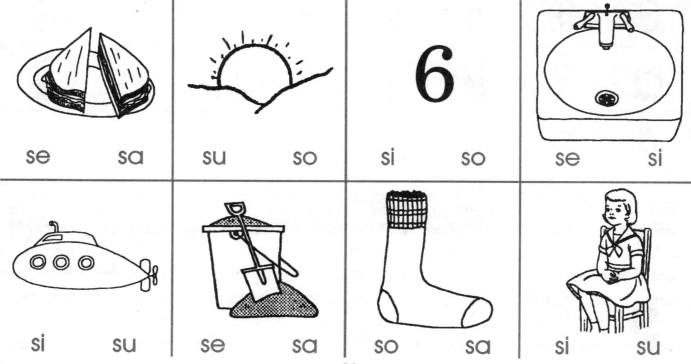

se sa	su so	si so	se si
si su	se sa	so sa	si su

Consonant Sound t -T

The next consonant to learn is **T - t** as in turtle. Look and listen for that sound as you say the names of these pictures. Circle the word if it begins with **t**. Cross out the other pictures.

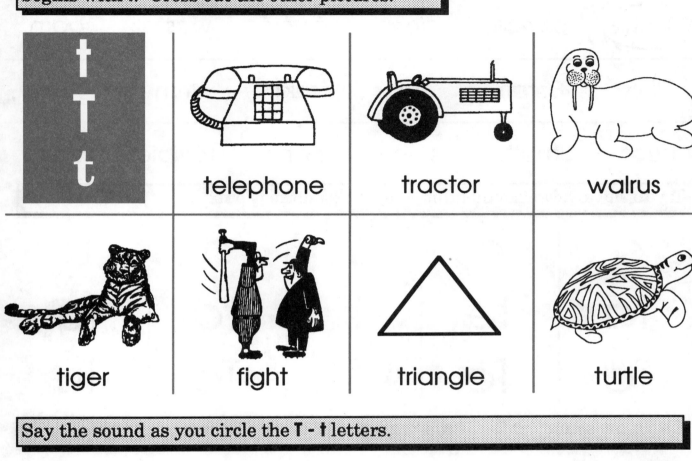

| | telephone | tractor | walrus |
| tiger | fight | triangle | turtle |

Say the sound as you circle the **T - t** letters.

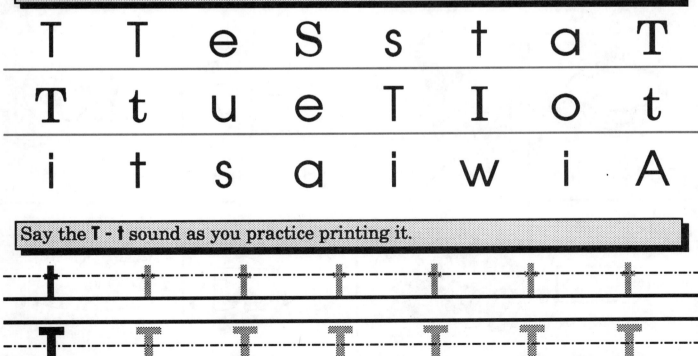

T   T   e   S   s   t   a   T

T   t   u   e   T   I   o   t

i   t   s   a   i   w   i   A

Say the **T - t** sound as you practice printing it.

Many words begin with the consonant **T - t**. Some of the words are below. Circle only the ones that begin with **T - t**.

(Tom)   ostrich   tree   truck   waste   barn

Tina   Sarah   egg   tough   trim   ten

---

treat   Timothy   silver   enter   terrible   trust

Try to say a vowel sound after you have said the **t** sound.

a	e	i	o	u
ta	**te**	**ti**	**to**	**tu**
Ta	Te	Ti	To	Tu

Circle the sound that is at the beginning of these pictures.

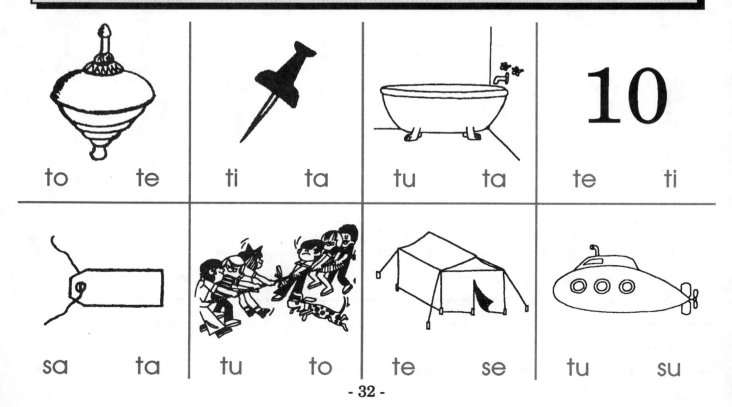

to te	ti ta	tu ta	te ti
sa ta	tu to	te se	tu su

Consonant Sound b - B

Circle only the words that begin with the sound of **B - b** as in Bible. Cross out the other words. Be sure to listen to the **B - b** sound.

| | Bible | barn | tree |
| banana | beaver | dolphin | bear |

Say the sound as you circle the **B - b** letters.

B	b	b	e	s	t	T	i
b	B	s	s	U	i	a	b
T	S	b	b	b	B	I	B

Say the **B - b** sound as you practice printing it.

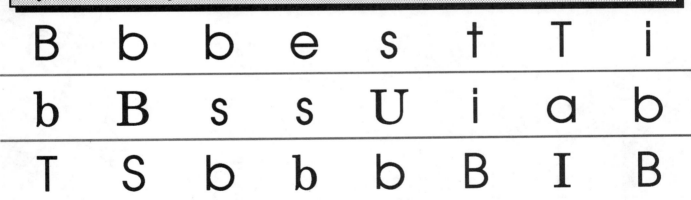

b b b b b b b

B B B B B B B

Circle the beginning B - b and short vowel that you hear in these words.

ba bi	be bu	be bo	bo bi
bo bu	be bi	be bu	bo ba

Which consonant do you hear at the beginning of these pictures?

s t b	s t b	s t b	s t b	s t b
s t b	s t b	s t b	s t b	s t b

Consonant Sound h -H

This page teaches the sound of **H - h** as in horse. If you hear and see that sound at the beginning of these words, circle the word. Cross out the other pictures.

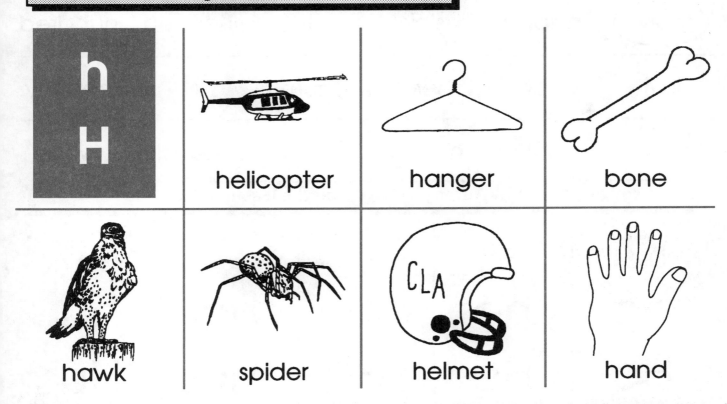

| h H | helicopter | hanger | bone |
| hawk | spider | helmet | hand |

Circle the consonant sound you hear at the beginning of these words.

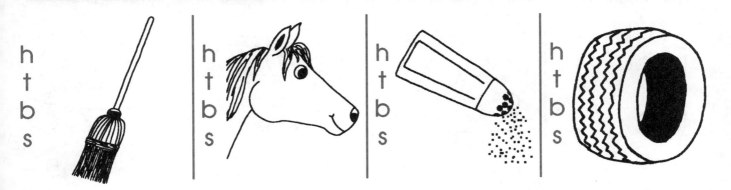

h
t
b
s

h
t
b
s

h
t
b
s

h
t
b
s

Say the **H - h** sound as you practice printing it.

h h h h h h h

H H H H H H H H

Circle only the words that begin with the **H - h** sound. Listen as your teacher reads them to you.

(holy)   happy   sick   it   heaven   hundred

hot   inch   hello   hum   no   healthy

hard   hospital   hungry   say   head   what

Try to say a vowel sound after you have said the **h** sound.

a	e	i	o	u
ha	he	hi	ho	hu
Ha	He	Hi	Ho	Hu

Circle the sound that is at the beginning of these pictures.

ha hi	he ho	hi ha	hu ha

s t b h	s t b h	s t b h	s t b h

Consonant Sound f - F

The sound of **F - f** is at the beginning of fox.
Circle the words that begin with the **F - f** sound.
Cross out the other words.

f F

flag

family

key

fire

pirate

fern

house

Say the sound as you circle the **F - f** letters.

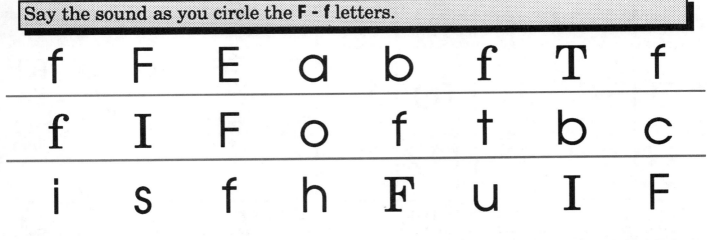

f F E a b f T f

f I F o f t b c

i s f h F u I F

Say the **F - f** sound as you practice printing it.

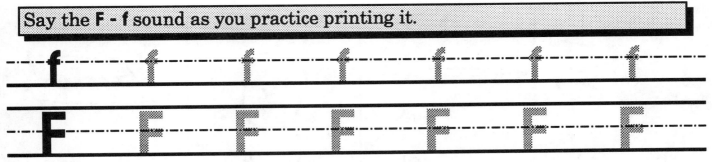

Adventures in Phonics - Level A

Circle the consonant sound you hear at the beginning of these words.

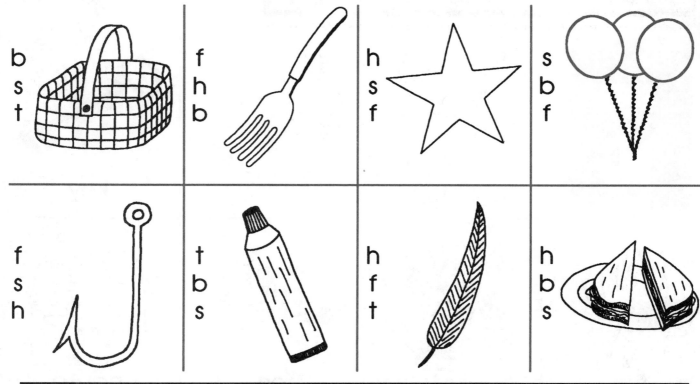

b s t | f h b | h s f | s b f

f s h | t b s | h f t | h b s

Practice saying these sounds.

a	e	i	o	u	fa fe fi fo fu
fa	fe	fi	fo	fu	Fa Fe Fi Fo Fu
Fa	Fe	Fi	Fo	Fu	

Think carefully as you try to read and circle the correct word.

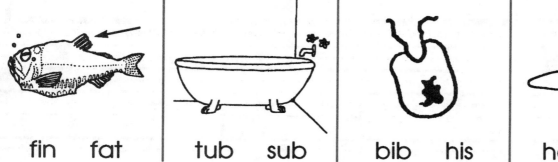

fin   fat | tub   sub | bib   his | hat   bus

Consonant Sound m -M

This page teaches the sound of **M** - **m** as in monkey. Carefully listen and look for that letter sound by the pictures and circle those words. Cross out the others.

| **m** **M** | mountains | gavel | money |
| mouse | vacuum | mailbox | monkey |

Say the sound as you circle the **M** - **m** letters.

M	f	s	m	s	m	N	f
F	m	M	h	I	n	o	M
B	h	m	t	n	M	s	m

Say the **M** - **m** sound as you practice printing it.

m m m m m m m m

M M M M M M M M

Many words begin with the sound of **M - m**.
Circle the ones you see in this part. Listen as
your teacher reads them to you.

(master)   come   music   magnet   mine   foreign

moon   mighty   trust   smile   book   move

manger   mustard   measure   me   maiden   my

muscle   melody   safely   major   James   candy

Do you still remember the other consonants you have learned?

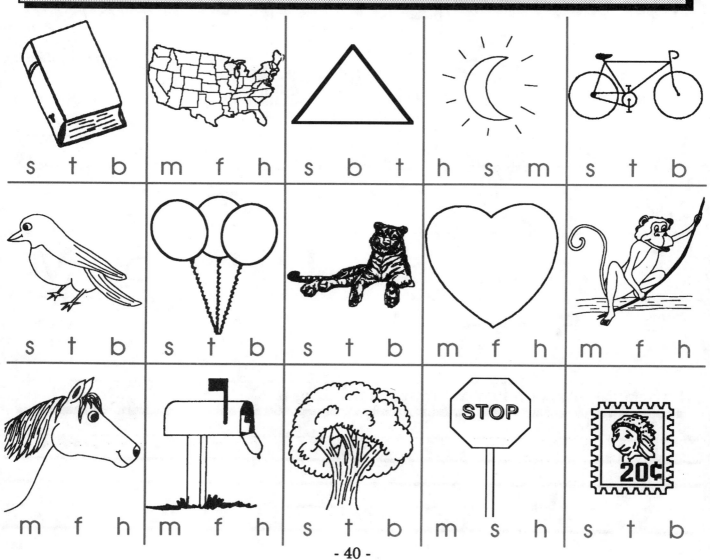

s t b   m f h   s b t   h s m   s t b

s t b   s t b   s t b   m f h   m f h

m f h   m f h   s t b   m s h   s t b

Consonant Sound c -C and k - K

This page teaches the **k** sound that both **C** - **c** and **K** - **k** make. The two letters share the work of the **k** sound. The **C** - **c** usually works with **a**, **o** and **u**. The **K** - **k** usually works with **e** and **i**.

c C	cat	king	k K
kite	turtle	corn	key

Say the sound as you circle the **C** - **c** and **K** - **k** letters.

K m C k s c K f

c k K C c e b L C

Say the **C** - **c** and **K** - **k** sound as you practice printing it.

C C C C C c c c

k k k k k k k k

k k k k k k k k

Adventures in Phonics - Level A

| Practice saying these sounds five times or more. Do you realize that this is how you begin to read? | |

a	e	i	o	u
ca	ke	ki	co	cu
Ca	Ke	Ki	Co	Cu

Do you still remember the other consonants you have learned? Circle the sound you hear at the beginning of these words.

s t c	m f h	c s t	f c h	k t s
b m f	h c t	k b m	f c k	m h f
mi ma	mi ca	ca fi	cu ti	hi fa

- 42 -

Consonant Sound d - D

Many of these pictures begin with the sound of **D - d** as in duck. Circle those words and cross out the other words.

dress	computer	door
dime	domino	ark	dog

Try to say a vowel sound after you have said the **d** sound.

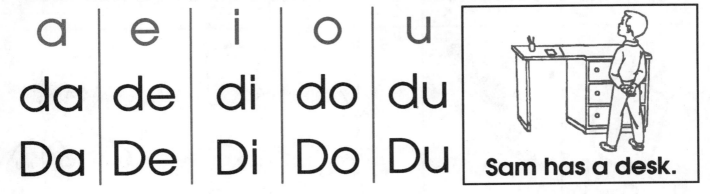

a	e	i	o	u
da	de	di	do	du
Da	De	Di	Do	Du

Sam has a desk.

Say the **D - d** sound as you practice printing it.

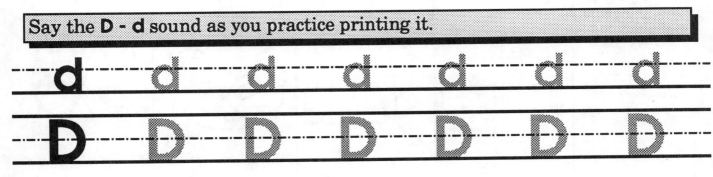

d d d d d d d

D D D D D D D

- 43 -

Color the pictures that begin with **D - d** as in duck.

Circle the sound you hear at the beginning of these words.

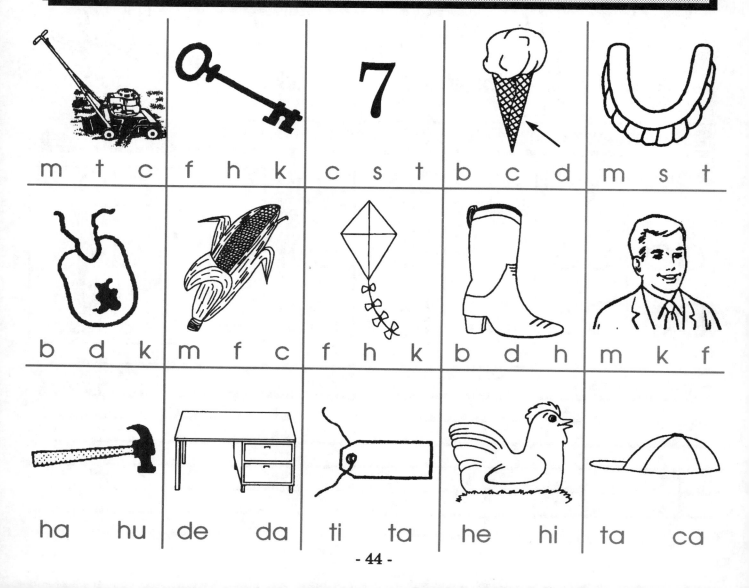

Consonant Sound j - J

The consonant on this page is the sound of **J - j** as in jaguar. Circle the word if you hear the **J - j** sound at the beginning. Cross out the other words.

j **J**	jet	jacks	jar
jeep	jump	knife	wagon

Say the sound as you circle the **J - j** letters.

J	i	o	j	j	I	d	j
u	J	s	t	h	k	j	s
j	j	J	f	J	b	J	j

Say the **J - j** sound as you practice printing it.

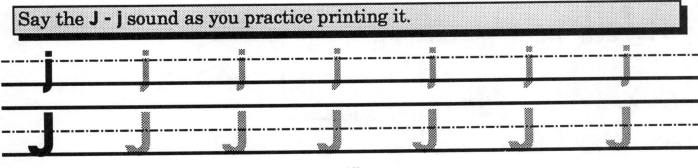

You have learned the sounds of many letters. Be careful as you think about the beginning sound in these pictures. Look at the letters in this box for help. **s t m j c k f h b d**

s

Circle the sound you hear at the beginning of these words.

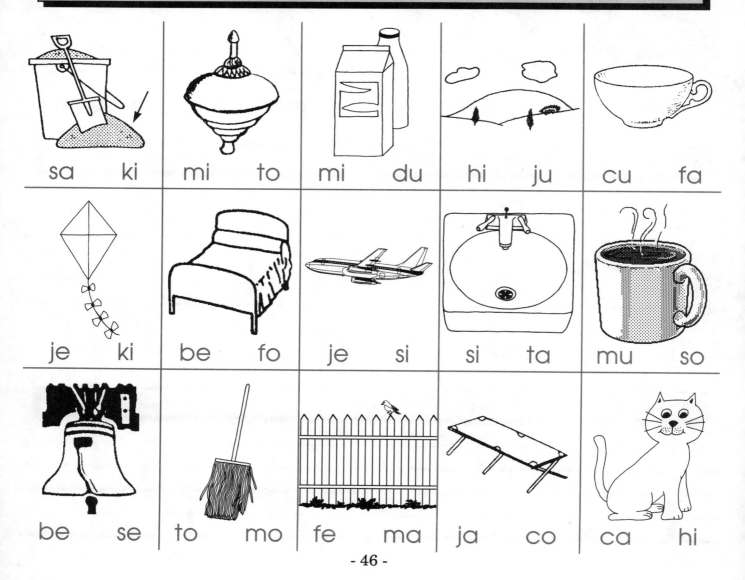

sa ki	mi to	mi du	hi ju	cu fa
je ki	be fo	je si	si ta	mu so
be se	to mo	fe ma	ja co	ca hi

The consonant on this page is the sound of **R - r** as in rabbit. Circle the word if you hear the **R - r** sound at the beginning. Cross out the other words.

| r R | ruler | rainbow | owl |

| ring | rat | men | rabbit |

Draw a line from the word to the correct picture.

rat

bat

cat

duck

rock

sock

Say the R - r sound as you practice printing it.

r r r r r r r

R R R R R R R

Adventures in Phonics - Level A

How thankful we should be to God for making our wonderful ears. They help us to hear which letter to circle to tell the beginning sounds of these pictures.

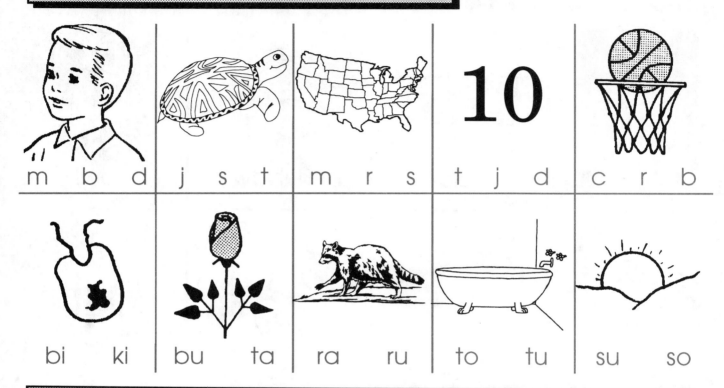

m b d   j s t   m r s   t j d   c r b

bi ki   bu ta   ra ru   to tu   su so

Now use your wonderful ears to listen for the ending sound in these words.

r m   t f   s k   t f

t k   b r   b d   t k

Color the words beginning with the sound of **G** - **g** as in goose. Notice how a typewriter may print the **g**.

| g G g | goat | gate | train |
| football | grasshopper | girl | goose |

Say the sound as you circle the **G** - **g** letters.

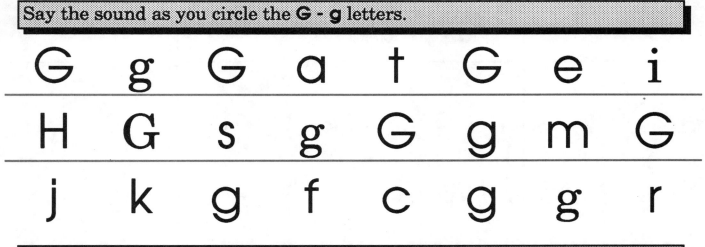

G g G a t G e i

H G s g G g m G

j k g f c g g r

Say the **G** - **g** sound as you practice printing it.

g g g g g g g g

G G G G G G G G

Circle all the words that begin with G - g. Listen as your teacher reads them.

(God)   game   glad   Tom   pen   jug

gold   Gospel   silver   go   gull   goodies

boy   grass   Grace   get   garden   foam

goat   sunshine   faith   when   clock   guest

Circle the beginning sound or the word which matches the picture.

f h g

b d c

d f g

t j c

d h g

h j c

k m s

h b s

gas   gift

bus   bug

tug   bag

gum   got

- 50 -

Consonant Sound l - L

Many words begin with the consonant **L - l** as in lion. Circle the **L - l** words and cross out the others.

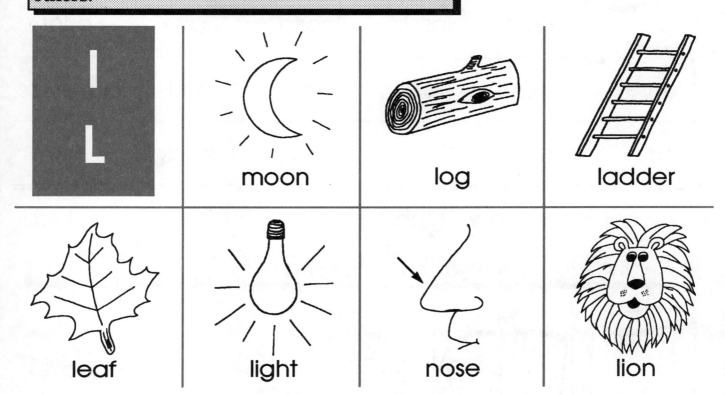

I l	moon	log	ladder
leaf	light	nose	lion

Draw a line from the word to the correct picture.

leg

list

lid

hill

bell

doll

Say the **L - l** sound as you practice printing it.

Adventures in Phonics - Level A

Circle all the words that begin with L - l. Listen carefully as they are read to you.

(Lord)   seeds   lamb   licorice   lake   print

cattle   lawn   sit   the   will   lollipop

laugh   lumber   love   life   luggage   teach

The   Lord   is   my   light.   I   will   love   the   Lord.

Circle the correct word which matches the picture.

bag bug | hem mug | bed bud | hill mill | tub rub

tug tag | cat cot | had sad | lock clock | list hat

tell bell | gas has | leg let | dots doll | milk silk

Now **N - n** is our next new sound. Color each word that begins with the **N - n** sound and cross out the others.

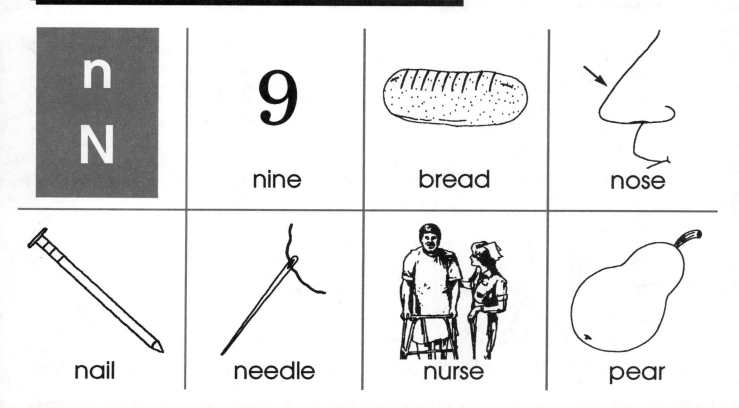

n N	9 nine	bread	nose
nail	needle	nurse	pear

Try to say a vowel sound after you have said the **n** sound.

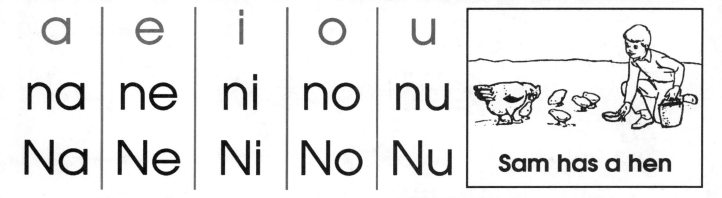

a	e	i	o	u
na	ne	ni	no	nu
Na	Ne	Ni	No	Nu

Sam has a hen

Say the **N - n** sound as you practice printing it.

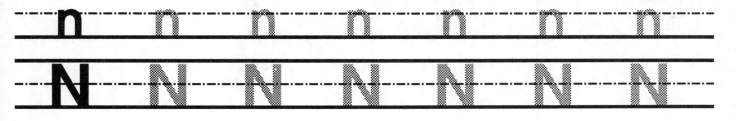

n n n n n n n n

N N N N N N N N

Look at the picture and carefully sound out the words. Circle the word which matches the picture.

nut run	nab neck	gas nest	ten tell	can tan
bed Ned	man tan	jam dim	not nest	pin fox

Listen for the ending sound in these words.

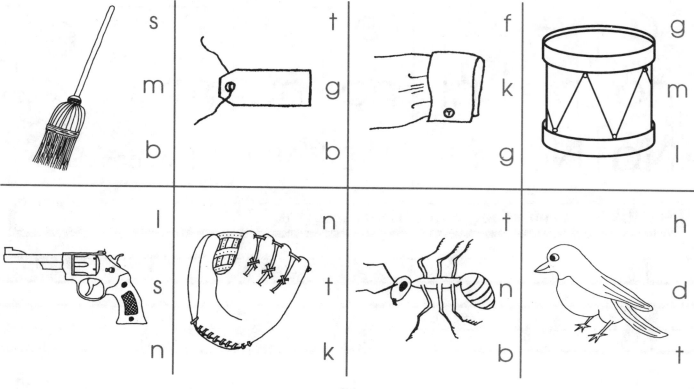

Will you **watch** for the **words** **w**hich begin **with** the sound of **W** - **w** as in **walrus**? Circle them and cross out the other **words**.

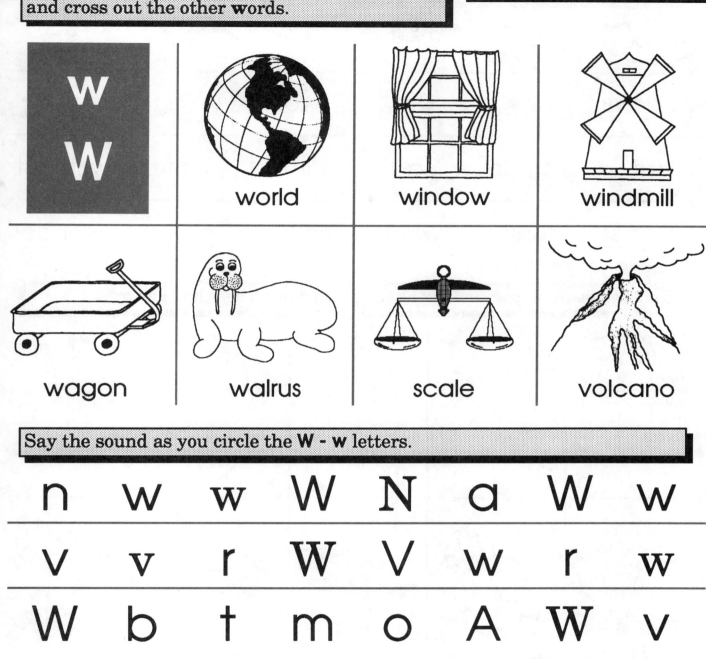

W **w**	world	window	windmill
wagon	walrus	scale	volcano

Say the sound as you circle the **W** - **w** letters.

n w w W N a W w

v v r W V w r w

W b t m o A W v

Say the **W** - **w** sound as you practice printing it.

w w w w w w w

W W W W W W W

Adventures in Phonics - Level A

Circle all the words that begin with **W** - **w**.
Listen as your teacher reads them.

(wood)   hot   west   water   will   star

wisdom   why   war   wall   wag   win

eat   worship   east   lamb   winter   without

weather   tent   wool   flower   crown   wonder

Circle the beginning sound or the word which matches the picture.

n w b	d k b	t r j	k h g	l w c
w l b	h f j	r t s	m k d	r n w
well tell	set web	gas mitt	mug fill	wag tag

- 56 -

Consonant Sound p - P

Circle the words that begin with the sound of **P - p** as in peacock. Cross out the other words.

penguin

pilgrim

scepter

pumpkin

pencil

zebra

puzzle

Draw a line from the word to the correct picture.

pin

pen

pond

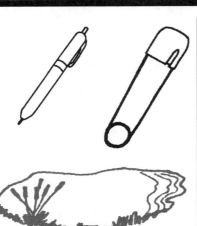

lock

duck

block

Say the **P - p** sound as you practice printing it.

p p p p p p p p p

P P P P P P P P P

- 57 -

Circle the words that begin with **P - p**. They are food for us. Listen as your teacher reads the words to you. Are you hungry now?

(peas)   peanuts   popcorn   parsley   corn   potato

meat   soup   pizza   pop   apple   orange

pickle   onion   squash   pear   punch   cracker

plum   carrot   pie   banana   parsnips   candy

Circle the sound or the word which matches the picture.

n b c	d k m	g l w	p g l	b s r
hum drum	flag jug	wag plug	pan fan	gum leg
sit pin	pit bug	fin pin	well can	gas pet

This page teaches the sound of **V - v** as in vulture. God made this bird in a very special way. Circle all the words that begin with the sound of **V - v** and cross out the other words.

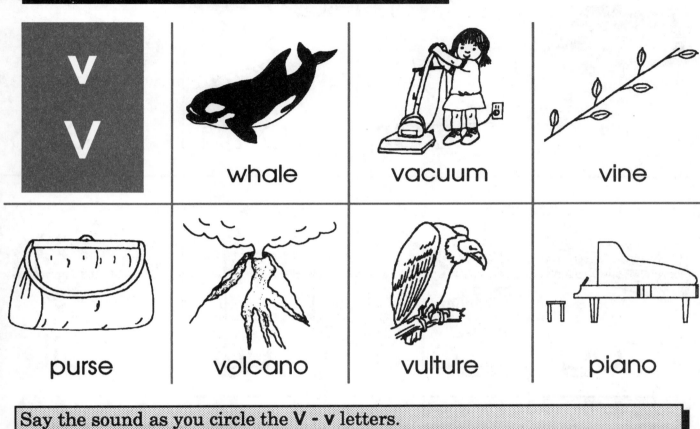

whale   vacuum   vine

purse   volcano   vulture   piano

Say the sound as you circle the **V - v** letters.

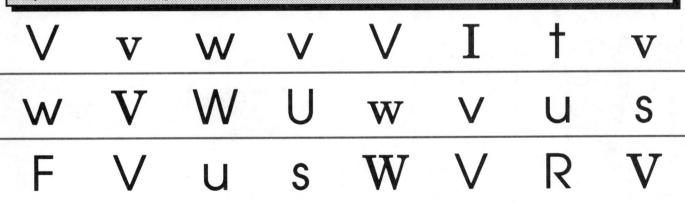

V v w v V I t v

w V W U w v u s

F V u s W V R V

Say the **V - v** sound as you practice printing it.

Print the missing sound at the beginning of each word.

___a n   ___ear   ___orm   ___et

___og   ___ake   ___ug   ___all

Listen for the ending sound in these words.

f   n   l   g
b   r   b   m
d   f   k   p

l   n   t   h
r   t   n   d
n   k   b   t

The sound of **Q - q** as in **qu**ail is **qu**ite interesting. It always has the **u** next to it. They make the same sound as **k - w**. Circle the words that begin with **qu**.

queen

pie

question

quilt

quill

newspaper

quarter

Say the sound as you circle the **Qu - qu** letters.

qu bi do qu qo qu Oe

Qe Bo pa Qe go ti qu

pa qu qu qa Ge Qo pa

Say the **Qu - qu** sound as you practice printing it.

qu qu qu qu qu qu qu

Qu Qu Qu Qu Qu Qu Qu

After you have circled all the **Qu - qu** words, listen as someone reads them to you.

_____

(quack)	kiss	quit	guess	guilt	honey
pail	quick	great	quest	quilt	music
quote	quartz	quality	queen	pit	pill
quarter	puff	quail	pin	quiz	quill

Circle the sound or the word which matches the picture.

qu d r	v k j	g l w	p g qu	l n m
p m t	f g j	w h p	p f k	s f l
gift lamp	sock pen	fuss bus	quill fill	jet jack

Consonant Sound y - Y

You now will learn the sound of **Y - y** as in yak. Listen closely to this sound. Circle the correct words and cross out the others.

yoke

yoyo

yell

yam

yarn

blouse

hoe

Say the sound as you circle the **Y - y** letters.

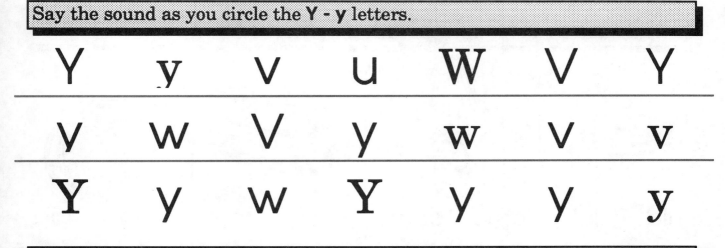

Y   y   v   u   W   V   Y

y   w   V   y   w   v   v

Y   y   w   Y   y   y   y

Say the **Y - y** sound as you practice printing it.

y   y   y   y   y   y   y   y

Y   Y   Y   Y   Y   Y   Y   Y

Print the missing sound at the beginning of each word.

9

 ___ine

 ___arn

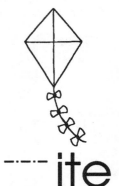 ___ree

 ___ite

 ___urse

 ___ake

 ___oyo

 ___ave

Circle the correct word which matches the picture.

 hid   lid

 lamp   camp

 van   tan

 mug   rug

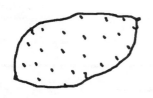 Sam   yam

 melt   quilt

 top   pup

 yell   well

Consonant Sound x - X

The sound of **X - x** is made by saying the sounds of **k** and **s**. The **X - x** is usually at the end of words. Circle each word that **ends** with the **X - x** and cross out the others.

	ax	ox	6 six
boat	wax	bank	box

Say the sound as you circle the **X - x** letters.

X   x   X   v   t   z   k

S   x   y   x   w   X   x

x   v   W   w   y   Z   K

Say the **X - x** sound as you practice printing it.

x   x   x   x   x   x   x

X   X   X   X   X   X   X

- 65 -

Adventures in Phonics - Level A

Print the beginning sound of these pictures.

s

t

b

v

qu

n

d

m

k

r

j

h

f

g

l

c

Consonant Sound z - Z

The last consonant sound to learn is the **Z - z** as in zebra. Color only the **Z - z** words. Cross out the other words.

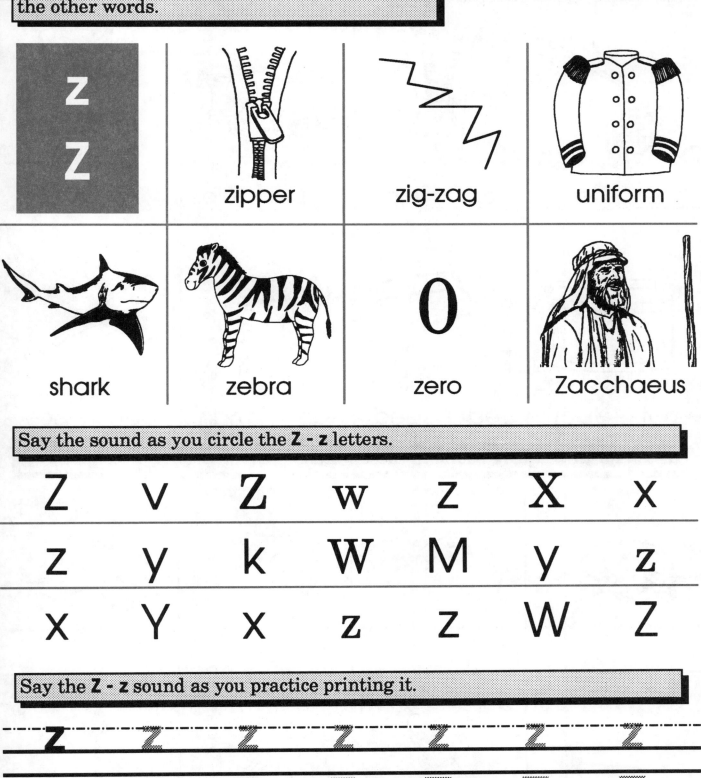

| | zipper | zig-zag | uniform |
| shark | zebra | zero | Zacchaeus |

Say the sound as you circle the **Z - z** letters.

Z v Z w z X x

z y k W M y z

x Y X z z W Z

Say the **Z - z** sound as you practice printing it.

z z z z z z z

Z Z Z Z Z Z Z

Adventures in Phonics - Level A

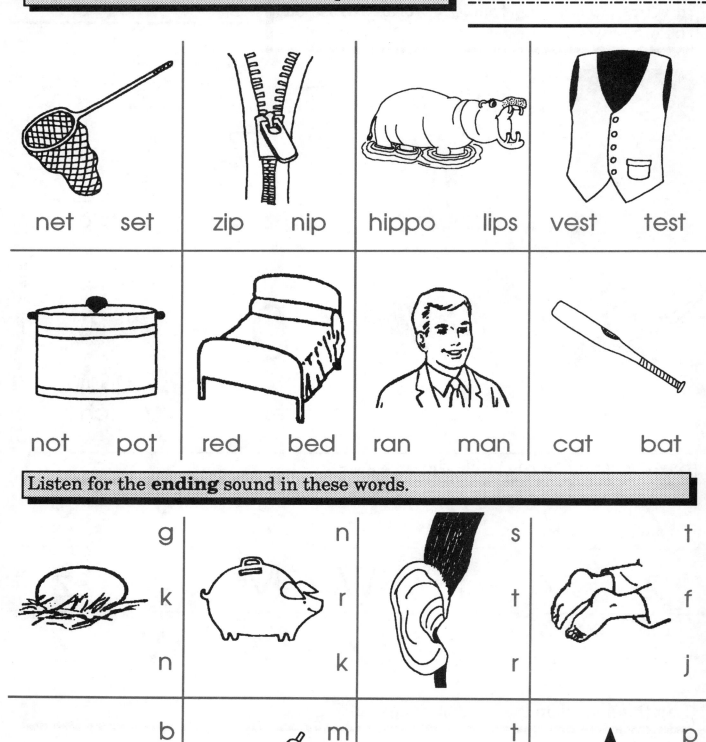

net set	zip nip	hippo lips	vest test
not pot	red bed	ran man	cat bat

Listen for the **ending** sound in these words.

g	n	s	t
k	r	t	f
n	k	r	j

b	m	t	p
r	n	n	d
g	s	x	t

- 68 -

Introducing Short Vowel - a - Words

These words have the short sound of **a**. Sound out the letters as you carefully trace the word. Draw a line to the correct picture in each group.

 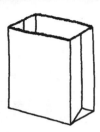  

map   bag   man   hat

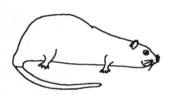   

van   rat   pan   ham

   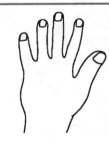

ant   hand   sand   sad

Read and trace the sentence. Color the picture when you are finished.

Sam has a bat.

These words have the short sound of **e**. Sound out the word as you trace it. Draw a line to the correct picture.

  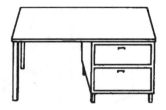

desk   well   ten   men

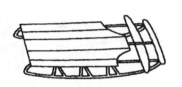   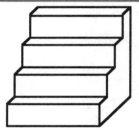

leg   sled   steps   net

  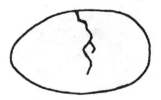 

left   smell   jet   egg

Read and trace the sentence. Color the picture when you are finished.

Jed has a pet hen.

Introducing Short Vowel - i - Words

This page has words with the short sound of i. Try to be careful as you trace each word. Draw a line to the correct picture.

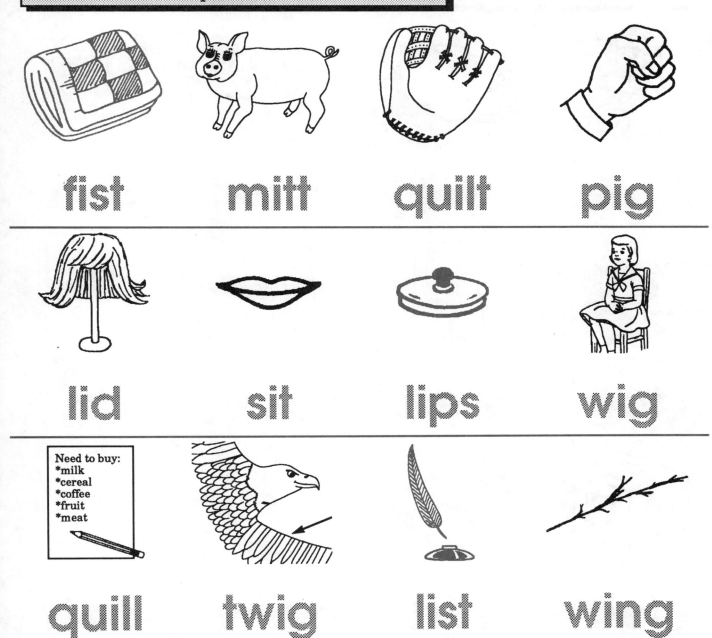

fist   mitt   quilt   pig

lid   sit   lips   wig

Need to buy:
*milk
*cereal
*coffee
*fruit
*meat

quill   twig   list   wing

Read and trace the sentence. Color the picture when you are finished.

The twins will sing.

This page has the short sound of **o** in the words. Do your very best work as you trace, sound out and draw the lines.

dots   doll   rock   stop

top   sock   lock   ox

   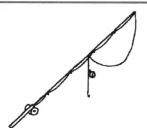

clock   rod   block   cot

Read and trace the sentence. Color the picture when you are finished.

Tom hops to the next box.

Introducing Short Vowel - u - Words

These words have the short sound of **u**. Sound out the word as you trace it. Draw a line to the correct picture.

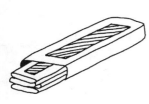   

rug **gum** **bus** **tub**

  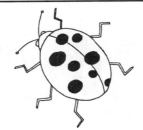 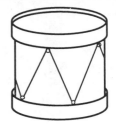

drum **cup** **run** **bug**

hump **club** **mug** **nut**

Read and trace the sentence. Color the picture when you are finished.

Jan hugs Dad.

Adventures in Phonics - Level A

Now you are ready to begin to read words!
Circle the correct word for each picture and
write it in the space below.

bat / can	map / gas	jam / bag	ran / man
hat / cab	ant / band	nap / tack	hand / pan
rat / sat	tag / wax	tan / van	hand / sand
ham / man	Jan / Sam	pat / ant	sad / had

Short Vowel - a - Words

Sam and Tom can see a big map.

pan				
cat				
cap				
tack	pan			
hand				
cast				
lamp				
man				
Sam				
wax				
bass				
back				

Think about each sound you hear in these words. Write the correct word in the space below.

pen hen	ten men	went tent	desk vest

10 | net ten | leg egg | steps wet | sell well |

sled web	leg peg	nest west	pet wet

Read the sentence and trace the words. Write the sentence a second time in the space below.

Ted can tell it is a bell.

Short Vowel - e - Words

Carefully print the correct word under each picture.

Dad and Sam see a cow next to the tent.

well desk net hen				
gem jet web vest				
bell pet wet bench				

- 77 -

Circle the correct word for each picture and write it in the space below.

mitt / fist	6 — six / mix	quilt / sill	fin / his
bib / hill	hill / mitt	lid / hid	zip / pin
lips / tip	milk / sit	hill / fill	quill / quilt
lift / gift	wig / twig	pin / twins	quill / wig

Short Vowel - i - Words

Carefully print the correct word under each picture.

Sam and Jan help pick up a big mess.

ring fin list quill			
wing pin mitt pig			
sing hit wig sink			

Think about each sound you hear in these words. Write the correct word in the space below.

_____

| doll | dots | box | mop |
| ox | pot | fox | hop |

| top | top | hop | cot |
| stop | rock | top | rod |

| sock | lock | hop | clock |
| lock | pot | pop | ox |

Read the sentences and carefully trace the words.

Jan has a doll.

The van will stop.

Short Vowel - o - Words

Carefully print the correct word under each picture.

Dad will tell Jan about God.

mop

dots

rod

cot

ox

clock

stop

block

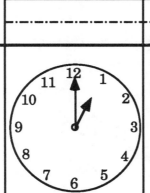

Read the sentences and carefully trace the words.

The sock is on the cot.

Mom has a big mop.

Adventures in Phonics - Level A

Think about each sound you hear in these words. Write the correct word in the space below.

pup / sun	cut / duck	tub / mug	hum / plug
bus / sun	jug / bug	hut / nut	bud / dug
jug / tug	gum / run	truck / duck	rug / tub
tug / plug	tuck / club	cut / sun	puff / cuff

- 82 -

Carefully print the correct word under each picture.

rug

bud

Wag is a pup. Can you find him?

up

run

tub

cuff

cup

jump

hug

suds

drum

sub

Think about each sound you hear in these words. Write the correct word in the space below.

pin / pat / pan	sit / map / cat	wag / tan / van	rag / rug / tag
rat / rag / sat	jam / sun / gas	cap / nut / lap	map / mitt / man
fan / ant / can	hand / run / sand	fit / duck / fan	camp / lamp / lips
bat / bag / pin	sat / bat / rat	fan / can / ran	tag / hand / lap

Words Having Short Vowels - a - e - i - o - u -

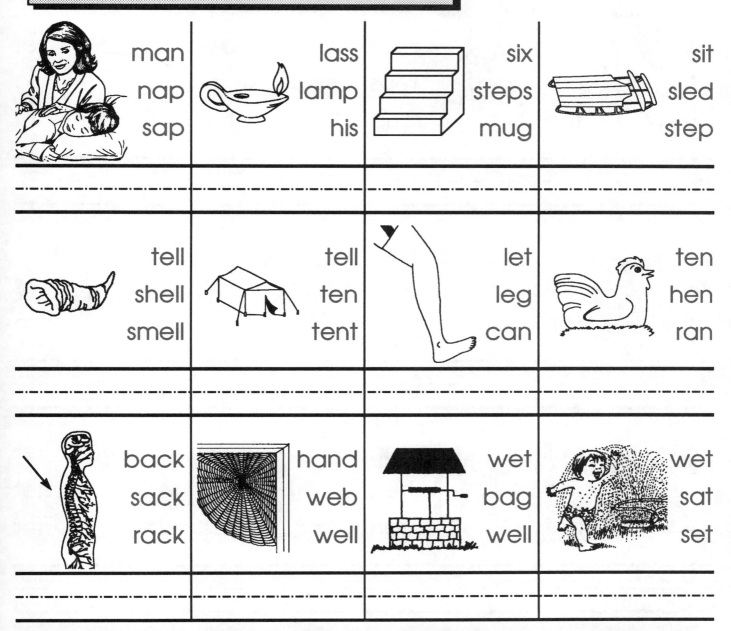

man	lass	six	sit
nap	lamp	steps	sled
sap	his	mug	step

tell	tell	let	ten
shell	ten	leg	hen
smell	tent	can	ran

back	hand	wet	wet
sack	web	bag	sat
rack	well	well	set

Read the sentence and trace the words. Write the sentence a second time in the space below.

Dad has a tan hat.

Adventures in Phonics - Level A

These words have either the short sound of **a** or **e**. Write the correct word in the space below.

vest / cat / ten	Sam / steps / mug	bet / jet / tan	get / egg / yam
let / pat / fan	web / well / glass	nest / rag / net	men / sat / ten
bell / bed / hat	ten / hen / ran	last / cast / past	set / met / net

Read the sentence and trace the words. Write the sentence a second time in the space below.

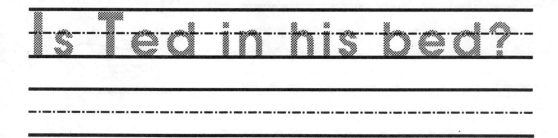 Is Ted in his bed?

Words Having Short Vowels - a - e - i - o - u -

These words have the short sound of **i** as in insect. Write the correct word in the space below.

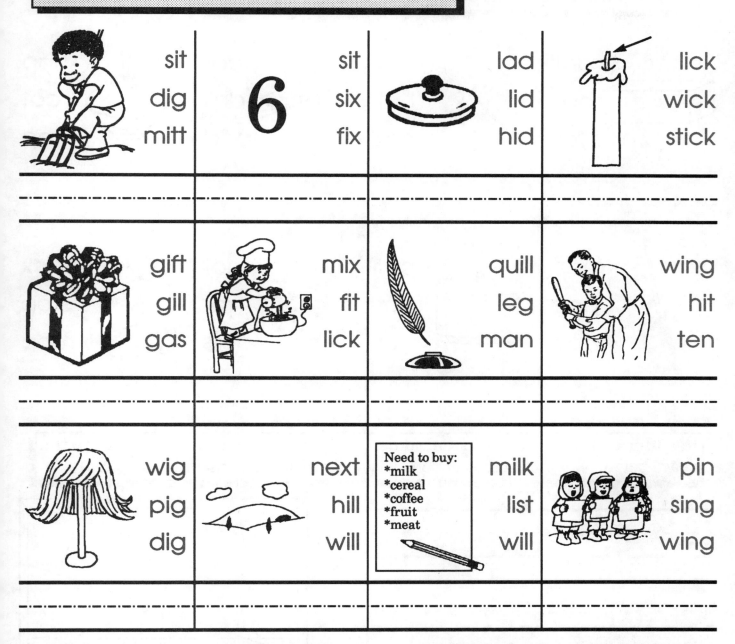

sit dig mitt	**6** sit six fix	lad lid hid	lick wick stick
gift gill gas	mix fit lick	quill leg man	wing hit ten
wig pig dig	next hill will	Need to buy: *milk *cereal *coffee *fruit *meat milk list will	pin sing wing

Read and trace the sentences. Color the picture when you are finished.

Sam can help his dad.

Sam can pick up a box.

Can you sound out these short o words? Write the correct word in the space below. God has given you a wonderful mind.

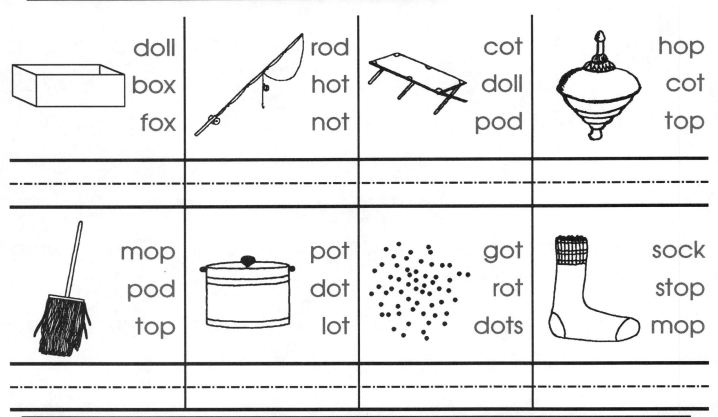

	doll		rod		cot		hop
	box		hot		doll		cot
	fox		not		pod		top

	mop		pot		got		sock
	pod		dot		rot		stop
	top		lot		dots		mop

Read the sentence and trace the words. Write the sentence a second time in the space below. Color only the sections with dots to discover the missing picture.

Find the dots.

God loves you.

Do you love God?

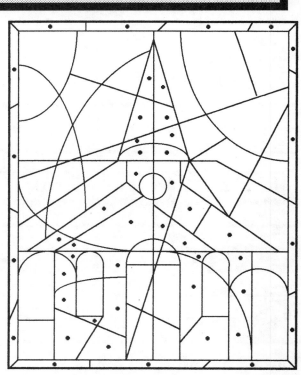

Words Having Short Vowels - a - e - i - o - u -

Can you sound out these short **u** words? Write the correct word in the space below. Try to do your very best work to honor God.

	sub		muff		cup		fall
	tub		cuff		pup		hall
	fun		club		rug		gull

	fun		gum		hunt		bus
	gun		drum		tug		fuss
	up		fun		mug		cuff

	hug		fuss		duck		pup
	fun		hut		club		jump
	run		bug		tub		rug

Read and trace the sentences. Color the picture when you are finished.

A duck is on the pond.

It can quack and quack.

Review 1
This page teaches how a short vowel in a word may be marked. See how the vowels are marked for the words in the box. As you do the work, <u>mark the vowel</u>, <u>read the word</u>, and <u>print it under the picture</u>. Then do the same for the next word.

| căt | běll | pĭn | fŏx | sŭn |

ĕgg

lock

map

pan

pen

pup

rug

sit

sock

ten

tent

van

Marking Short Vowels in Words

Review 2. Mark each vowel and carefully print the words under the correct pictures.

băg

clock

cuff

cup

desk

hump

jet

lamp

list

quill

twig

wĕb

Need to buy:
*milk
*cereal
*coffee
*fruit
*meat

Read and trace the sentences.

Bill has a quill in his hand.

The hen will rest in a nest.

Review 3. Mark each vowel and carefully print the words under the correct pictures.

bĭb

box

bug

doll

dots

mitt

mug

quilt

plug

stop

top

tŭb

Read and trace the sentences.

Jan has a muff and cap.

The sun is big and hot.

Marking Short Vowels in Words

Review 4. Mark each vowel and carefully print the words under the correct pictures.

ănt

cap

cot

drum

duck

gift

gum

rod

sand

steps

twins

wig

Read and trace the sentences.

A duck is on the pond.

Jon has a cap and drum.

Review 5. Some of the words are missing for the pictures. Can you sound out the letters as you print them?

bănk

bud

cast

clip

gas

hop

lift

sun

Read and trace the sentences.

Is there gas in the bus?

It is fun to hop and fish.

Spelling Short Vowel Words

On this page you will have to think carefully about the sounds in these words. Try to do your very best printing. Your parents will be happy.

duck

Is your pencil ready to go to work again? Try to write the correct name under each picture.

Will you color this jet red and black?

Spelling Short Vowel Words

Here comes another page without any helping words. Try to honor God as you do your assignment.

Will you hop on the bus with us?

Do you remember what to do on a page like this? Try to write the names of the pictures without any helping words.

Need to buy:
*milk
*cereal
*coffee
*fruit
*meat

Will you draw the pictures for these words?

bag	hill	sun	tent
cup	hat	egg	six

Consonant Blends

Many words begin with two or three consonants. When each of these consonants says its usual sound, we call it a blend. You have seen blends in such words as **bl**ock. Say the sound as you trace each blend and draw a line to the correct picture.

bl	cl	fl	gl	pl	sl

bl bl bl block

cl cl cl clock

fl fl fl flag

gl gl gl glass

pl pl pl plug

sl sl sl sled

Underline the blends as you sound out the words. Carefully print the words in the correct spaces.

clip

flag

sled

glasses

These words begin with the **r** blends. Practice saying them many times.

| br | cr | dr | fr | gr | pr | tr |

br   br   br   brick

cr   cr   cr   crab

dr   dr   dr   drum

fr   fr   fr   frog

gr   gr   gr   grass

pr   pr   pr   print

tr   tr   tr   truck

Circle the correct word which matches the picture.

brick	drip		grip
trick	dress		trip
track	drop		drip
grass	brick		grab
grip	brag		crab
grin	bring		drum

Consonant Blends

Brad will print at his desk.

flag drum block plug	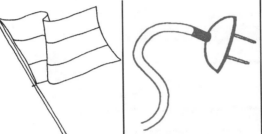	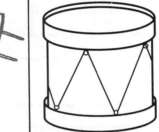		
truck glass clock plant				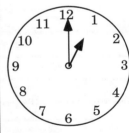

Read the sentence and carefully trace the words.

The truck got stuck.

The rat got in a trap.

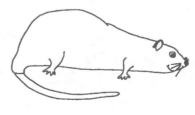

rat

These words begin with the **s** blends. Practice saying them many times.

sc	sk	sm	sn	sp	st	sw

sc   sc   sc   scrub

sk   sk   sk   skip

sm   sm   sm   smell

sn   sn   sn   snake

sp   sp   sp   spin

st   st   st   steps

sw   sw   sw   swim

Circle the correct word which matches the picture.

	skip steps smell		snap scab skip		spill spit spin
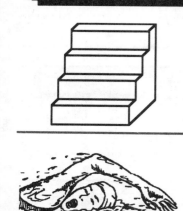	swim skill snap		smell spin swim		steps still stop

Consonant Blends

dw	squ	tw

dw dw dw dwell

squ squ squ square

tw tw tw twins

Think as you underline the beginning blend and carefully print it under the correct picture.

clip

dwell

flag

scab

smell

stamp

twig

twins

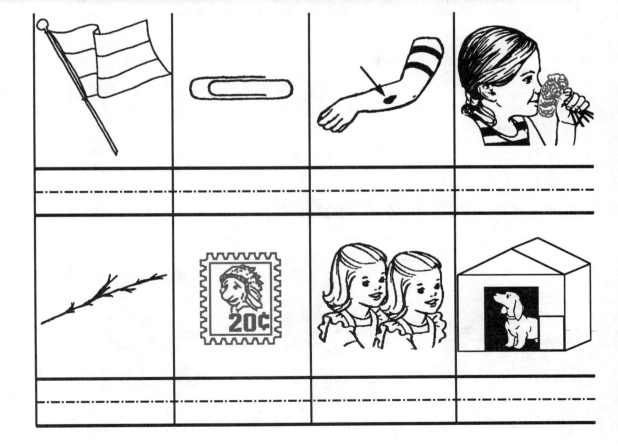

These blends have three consonants. Practice saying them until you know them. Say them each time you print them.

scr	spl	spr	str

scr scr scr scrub

spl spl spl splash

spr spr spr spring

str str str strap

Circle the triple blend that you hear at the beginning of these pictures.

scr spr str	spl scr spr	scr str spl	spl str scr

str spl scr	spl scr spr	str spl scr	str spl scr

Consonant Blends

blast

clock

crab

drink

grass

print

prison

stamp

swim

tractor

tree

twelve

12

Sam can swim fast.

Tom has a clip.

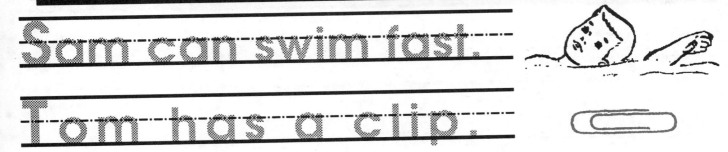

When a word has a **short vowel sound**, usually the consonants **s**, **l**, **f**, and **z** will be doubled. Double consonant words, such as hill, doll and dress, have been in previous lessons. Some exceptions to the doubling rule are bus, gas, yes, as, is, has, was and his. Underline the double consonant and print the word next to the picture.

cuff

bell

kiss

glass

quill

dress

well

mitt

Say these words as you print them. Notice the ending double consonants.

miss mess bass muss fuss

doll sell pill dull will

puff sniff staff cliff stuff

buzz fuzz fizz spill muff

Words Ending with ss, ll, ff, zz and ck

Remember that these short vowel sounds words end with double consonants if they end with **l**, **f**, **s** or **z**. Practice reading these words as you print them.

ll	**ff**	**ss**	**zz**
doll	cuff	miss	fuzz
fell	stiff	less	fizz
still	staff	pass	buzz
dull	huff	fuss	jazz

Underline the double consonant and print the word under the picture.

pill

smell

yell

doll

hill

buzz

bass

well

Another set of letters that belong with the **ss**, **ll**, **ff** and **zz**, is the **ck**. Whenever a short vowel sound word ends with a **k** sound, it is the **ck** that must be there. Many of these words have been in previous lessons.

sŏ<u>ck</u>				
lock				
rock				
lick				
brick				
wick				
jack				
track				
block				
back				
tack				
kick				

Read the sentences and carefully trace the words.

The duck says quack.

Pick up the stick.

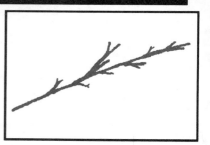

Words Ending with ss, ll, ff, zz and ck

This is a review of the five double letters:
ss   ll   ff   zz   ck

quill

doll

bell

glass

block

press

gull

bass

How much have you learned? Can you spell these words without help?

The **sk**, **sp** and **st** blends may be at the **end** of some **short vowel sound** words. Mark the short vowel, underline the ending consonant blends and print each word carefully.

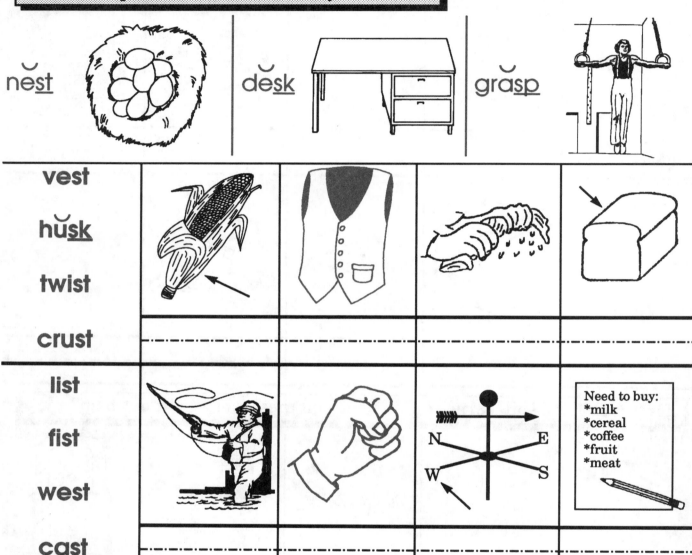

nĕ<u>st</u>

dĕ<u>sk</u>

gră<u>sp</u>

vest

husk

twist

crust

list

fist

west

cast

Learn to read these words as you print them. Say them several times.

rest   fast   risk   wisp   gasp

Jen will ask Jan to rest.

Jan has a cast.

Words Ending with Consonant Blends

These **short vowel sound** words end with lf, lk, lp and lt. Mark the short vowel, underline the ending consonant and carefully print the words.

belt

mĕl̲t̲

milk

help

wilt

elk

tilt

quilt

These **short vowel sound** words end with **mp** and **nd**. Follow the directions at the top of the page.

band

hăn̲d̲

sand

pond

hump

stamp

jump

lamp

Many **short vowel sound** words end with two consonants. Underline the **ct, ft, nt, pt** or **xt** as you see them at the end of these words. Mark the short vowel and neatly print the word under the picture.

tĕ<u>nt</u>	$\begin{array}{r} 3 \\ +\underline{2} \\ 5 \end{array}$			
fact				
wept				
gift				
left		Proverbs 3:5-6 5. Trust in the LORD with all thine heart; and lean not unto thine own understanding. 6. In all thy ways acknowledge Him, and He shall direct thy paths.		? right
hunt				
slant				
text				

Say these words as you print them. Notice the ending double consonants.

sent went bent rent dent

kept slept crept duct act

next swift drift hunt lift

An ant will drift on the raft.

Words Ending with Consonant Blends

In previous lessons you learned the words **sing** and **wing**. Listen closely to the ending consonant sounds as you say these words. The **ng** consonants make a special sound that is not the same as when **n** and **g** are separate. This lesson also teaches the **nk** sound as in **ink**. Mark the short vowel, underline the ending consonants and print the words.

sw**ing**

drink

trunk

sing

bank

wing

string

ring

Say these words as you print them.

pink blink mink tank crank

bang sang bring dunk

ding-dong ding-dong

The bell is ringing.

A consonant digraph has two consonants that make one sound. Two of the digraphs are **sh** as in ship and **ch** as in chin. These two digraphs may be at the beginning or end of a word. Say the sound as you trace them.

sh   sh   sh   sh   sh   sh   ship

ch   ch   ch   ch   ch   ch   chin

Circle the digraph and print the word carefully.

(ch)ick			
church			
check			
brush			
chimney			
bench			
splash			
fish			
ship			
chin			
branch			
bush			

Words with Digraphs ch, sh, th and wh

Do you remember what a digraph is? A consonant digraph has two consonants that make **one** sound as **sh**ip and **ch**in. Two more digraphs are **th** as in that, or **th** as in think, and **wh** as in whip. Can you hear the two different sounds of **th**? The first sound makes a noise, and the second makes a whisper. Say them several times. The **th** may be seen at the beginning, middle or end of words. After you have traced, have your teacher help you read these **th** words.

them   then   that   this   the

father   mother   brother

These words have the whisper sound of **th**.

with   thing   thank   think

The **wh** is at the beginning of these words.

when   which   whisk   whiff

Circle the correct beginning sound which matches the picture.

th wh	th wh	th wh
th wh	th wh	th wh

We have studied that when there is only one vowel in the middle of a word it has a short sound such as in cat, pen and box. This page teaches the long sound that the **A - a** makes. When two vowels are in a word, usually the first vowel says its name, and the second vowel is silent. Some words have **a_e** which means a consonant comes between the two vowels. Some of the words have **ai** in the middle. Study the first two rows. Look at and listen to the short and long **A - a** sounds in the words.

| a | e | i | o | u |

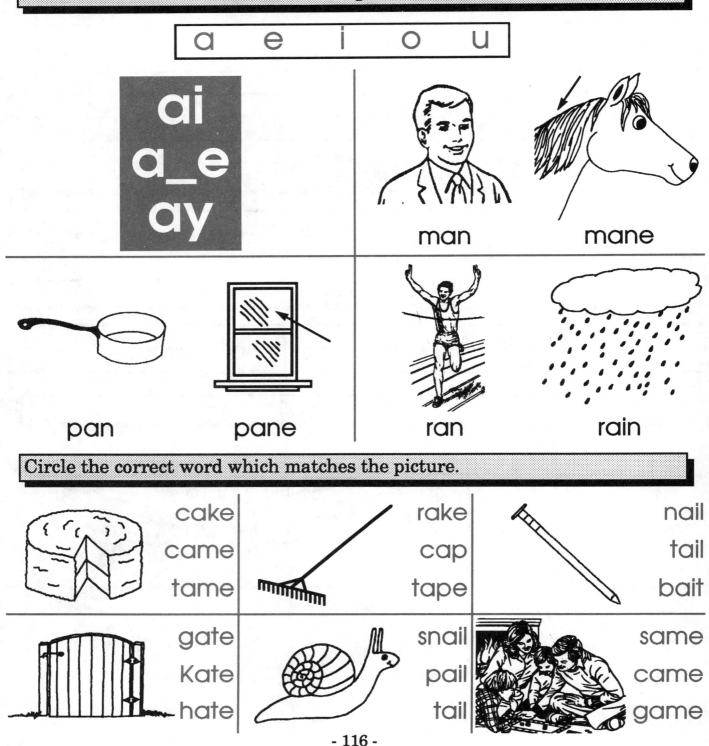

ai
a_e
ay

man   mane

pan   pane   ran   rain

Circle the correct word which matches the picture.

cake	rake	nail
came	cap	tail
tame	tape	bait

gate	snail	same
Kate	pail	came
hate	tail	game

Long Vowel - a - Words

The pup has a tail.

cake				
wave				
rake				
ape				

make				
sail				
gate				
pane				

vane				
mail				
cane				
lake				

In this lesson you will hear the long sound of **A - a**. Remember: when two vowels are in a word, usually the first vowel says its name, and the second vowel is silent. When **y** is at the end of a word, it is a vowel. On this page, **y** is silent because it comes after the **a**. Circle the correct word for each picture and write it in the space below.

vail / scale / tale	rake / cake / skate	make / came / nail	game / came / gate
tail / take / rain	sail / make / name	lake / make / bake	hail / rail / quail
mail / pail / hail	Kate / take / cane	pray / bait / say	bat / bait / nail

Read the sentence and carefully trace the words.

Kay gave Jane a game to play.

Long Vowel - a - Words

way				
mane				
ape				
pay				

rain				
save				
bait				
pail				

When **y** is at the end of a word, it acts as a vowel. If **y** comes after a vowel, the **y** is silent. In these words, the **a** says its name and the **y** is silent.

pray				
hay				
play				
spray				

Try to read these words. Will you read them three times?

| day | say | may | bay | jay | lay | hay | clay | ray | pay |

This lesson teaches how to mark long vowel words. Remember to think that the first vowel says its name, and the second vowel is silent. On the list mark the vowels in the word and then print the word under the picture. Then go back to the list and mark the vowels in the next word and print it.

cāke̸   pāi̸l   prāy̸

āpe̸

cake

game

gate

hay

mail

nail

pane

rain

rake

save

tail

nail

Put on your thinking cap as you do the work on this page. In the little box above each section you will see the vowels to use as you print. Remember to print a **k** if that sound comes before an **e** as in ca**k**e.

a_e

take

a i

a y

Jan is holding two words that rhyme. Can you read them? Words that rhyme have the same vowel sound and ending sound. Match these rhyming words by drawing a line between them.

save   bake

cake   wave

rain   play

tray   train

Fill in the missing letters to write more rhyming words to read.

pay	**sail**	**lake**	**game**
pr _ _	f _ _ _	b _ _ _	f _ _ _
d _ _	G _ _ _	c _ _ _	fl _ _ _
b _ _	h _ _ _	t _ _ _	c _ _ _
h _ _	j _ _ _	f _ _ _	bl _ _ _
j _ _	m _ _ _	J _ _ _	l _ _ _
m _ _	n _ _ _	s _ _ _	n _ _ _
s _ _	p _ _ _	m _ _ _	s _ _ _
pl _ _	qu _ _ _	w _ _ _	t _ _ _
st _ _	r _ _ _	r _ _ _	sh _ _ _
w _ _	t _ _ _	qu _ _ _	fr _ _ _

Long Vowel - e - Words

These words have the long sound of **e** as in eagle. They have two vowels. The first vowel says its name, and the second vowel is silent. Some words have **ee** and some have **ea**. Circle the word which matches the picture and write it in the space.

e ea			
ee ey	tree tea sea	bet bed beads	seat wheat beat
	_____	_____	_____
3	tree wheat three	fear ear tear	feel feet well	queen quit quilt
	_____	_____	_____
	teeth week team	ship feet seal	reap east feet	team ear leaf
	_____	_____	_____

Read the sentences and carefully trace the words.

We eat meat with teeth.

God gave us ears to hear.

Remember to look at the vowels. The first vowel says its name, and the second vowel is silent.

leaf

peanut

teach

seat

sweep

peas

sheep

wheat

heel

deer

beak

key

When a word has only one vowel which is an **e** at the end of the word, it is a long vowel. Read the sentences and carefully trace the words.

He will teach me to read.

She sweeps so it will be clean.

This lesson teaches how to mark long vowel words. Remember to think that the first vowel says its name, and the second vowel is silent. On the list, mark the vowels in the word and then print the word under the correct picture. Repeat this process until you have used all the words in the list.

bēȧk   bēė   kēჯ

beȧds
ear
feet
key
meal
queen
reap
seal
teeth
three
tree
wheel

Adventures in Phonics - Level A

Think about how these words should be spelled. The vowels in the boxes will help you.

e a

e e

Do you still remember how to spell these short e words?

Long Vowel - e - Words

This page is a review of the long **a** and **e**. Will you carefully print the words under the correct picture.

pray

bee

pail

feet

nail

rain

cane

sweep

plane

ape

play

heel

Read the sentences and carefully trace the words.

May we pray each day.

God will hear and help us.

The vowels **ey** usually say the long vowel sound as in key. They also may say the long vowel sound of **a** as in they and obey. Match these rhyming words by drawing a line between them.

seam	wheel	tree	meat
fear	peak	bead	leap
feel	steam	heap	bee
leak	dear	beat	feed

Fill in the missing letters to write more rhyming words to read.

sh**eep**	s**eal**	s**eat**	b**ean**
d _ _ _	d _ _ _	b _ _ _	l _ _ _
j _ _ _	h _ _ _	n _ _ _	d _ _ _
k _ _ _	p _ _ _	h _ _ _	m _ _ _
w _ _ _	m _ _ _	wh _ _ _	cl _ _ _
sl _ _ _	r _ _ _	m _ _ _	gl _ _ _

Complete these sentences with the missing words found in the box.

They bee obey wave

1. See Jane _____ to Mother.
2. They hear the buzz of a _____.
3. God tells us to _____ His rules.
4. _____ will help us each day.

Long Vowel - i - Words

These words have the long sound of **i** as in ice. Most of the words have **i_e**. A couple of words have **ie**. You will soon learn that an ending **y** may also say the long **i** sound. Circle the word which matches the picture and write it in the space.

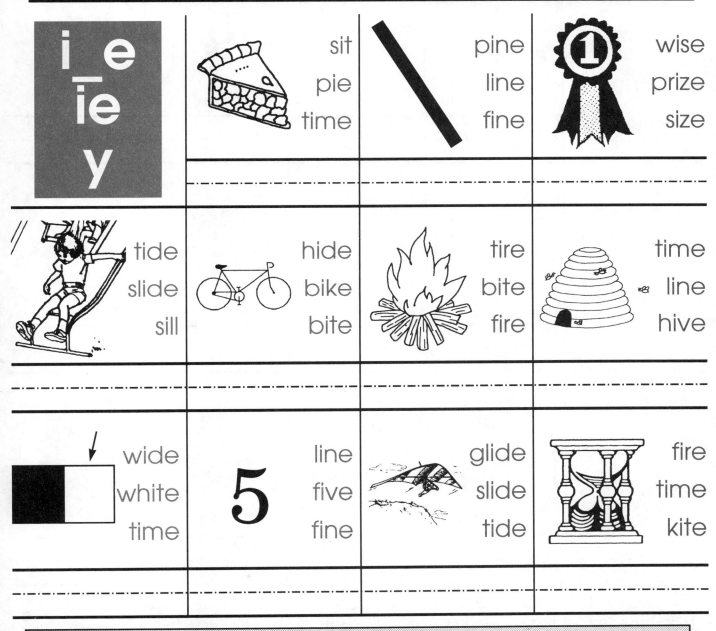

i̅e̅ / i̅e̅ / y	sit / pie / time	pine / line / fine	wise / prize / size
tide / slide / sill	hide / bike / bite	tire / bite / fire	time / line / hive
wide / white / time	line / five / fine	glide / slide / tide	fire / time / kite

Read the sentences and carefully trace the words.

Let us go for a bike ride.

Is it time to go to bed?

Remember, the first vowel says its name, and the second vowel is silent. Write the correct name under each picture.

prize

kite

nine

vine

five

dime

wires

tie

bite

tire

dive

drive

These words have only **y** as a vowel. When it is at the end of a word it says the long **i**. Circle the correct word which matches the picture.

cry
dry
fly

dry
shy
fry

cry
fly
dry

Long Vowel - i - Words

| fīvę | pīę | crȳ |

bīkę

dry

fire

glide

hive

kite

line

nine

slide

fly

time

white

Put your thinking cap on as you do the work on this page. In the little box above each section, you will see the vowels to use as you print. Remember to print a **k** if that sound comes before an **e** as in bike.

i_e

y

Do you still remember the short vowel sound of **i**?

Long Vowel - i - Words

tire	dive	file	time
five	shine	fly	bike
dry	wire	dime	sky
vine	try	hike	pile

kit	kite	dim	_____	rid	_____
rip	_____	fin	_____	Tim	_____
can	_____	mat	_____	cap	_____
bit	_____	mad	_____	at	_____
Jan	_____	tap	_____	man	_____
hat	_____	hid	_____	pan	_____

fire	pipe	five	bike

1. Mike likes to ride on his _____.
2. Dad will hire Ed to fix a _____.
3. We can feel the heat of the _____.
4. Jake has _____ black pens in a box.

These words have the long sound of **o** as in oak. They have two vowels. The first vowel says its name, and the second vowel is silent. Most of the words have **o_e** as in pole or **oa** as in boat. The **w** is a vowel when it follows another vowel. One of the sounds it makes is the long **o** as in mow.

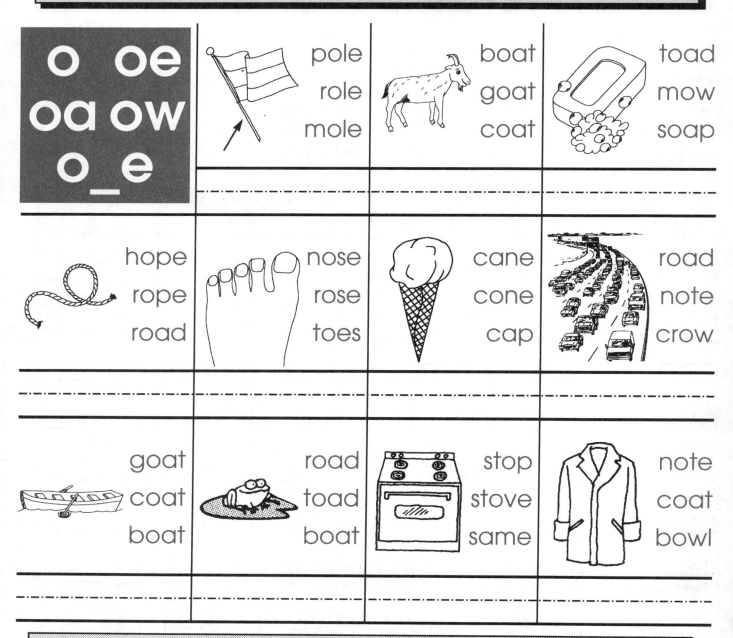

o oe			
oa ow			
o_e			

pole role mole	boat goat coat	toad mow soap
hope rope road	nose rose toes	cane cone cap	road note crow
goat coat boat	road toad boat	stop stove same	note coat bowl

The **ow** says a long **o** in these words. Try to read them as you trace.

crow snow tow bowl slow

May God bless this home.

Long Vowel - o - Words

toast			
home			
nose			
bone			
stove			
goat			
coal			
mow			
hoe			
bowl			
dome			
hose			
snow			
bow			
goal			
note			

This lesson teaches how to mark long vowel words. Remember to think that the first vowel says its name, and the second vowel is silent. On the list, mark the vowels in the word and then print the word under the correct picture. Repeat this process until you have used all the words in the list.

hōme̸   cōa̸t   dōe̸

bōa̸t

bow

coat

cone

blow

goal

note

pole

rope

toad

toe

yoke

Long Vowel - o - Words

o_e

oa

Do you still remember the short vowel sound of **o**?

Adventures in Phonics - Level A

Three sets of vowels make the long **o** vowel sound; they are **oa**, **o_e** and **ow**. Match these rhyming words by drawing a line between them.

toast   bone joke   show

cone   low   coat   poke

bow   pole home   foam

hole   roast snow   goat

Print the sets in the lists below and read the words.

oa   **o_e**   **ow**

t _ _ d   h _ s _   b _ _

r _ _ d   n _ s _   l _ _

t _ _ st   r _ s _   m _ _

b _ _ t   p _ s _   r _ _

Complete these sentences with the missing words found in the box.

nose stone hole bone rose hope toad

1. Joe can see a green _____ on a _____.

2. I think he may jump into the _____.

3. Can you see the toad's _____?

4. The toad will not eat the _____ and the _____.

5. I _____ the toad will go to my home with me.

- 138 -

Long Vowel - u - Words

These words have the long sound of **u**. The long **u** may sound like **u** as in suit or **yu** as in mule. The **ew** also makes the long **u** sound as in new. Circle the word which matches the picture and write it in the space.

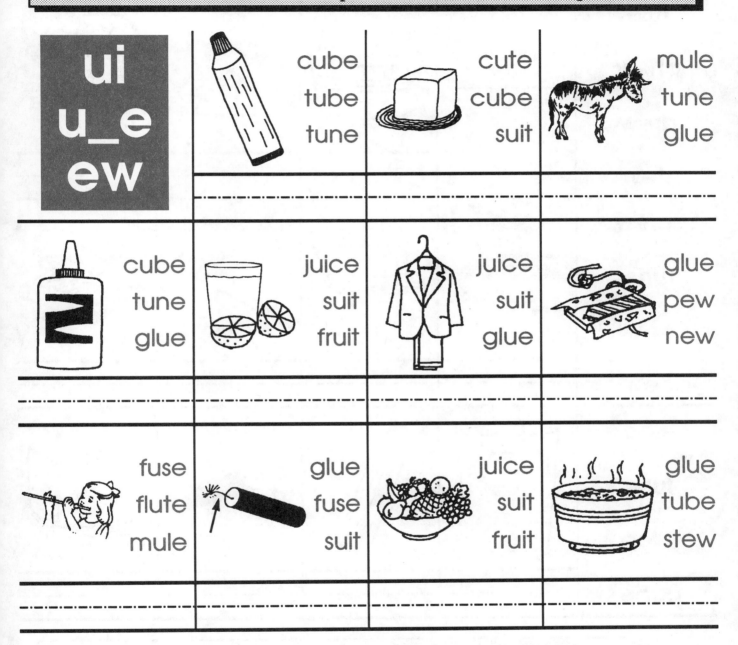

ui
u_e
ew

	cube		cute		mule
	tube		cube		tune
	tune		suit		glue

	cube		juice		juice		glue
	tune		suit		suit		pew
	glue		fruit		glue		new

	fuse		glue		juice		glue
	flute		fuse		suit		tube
	mule		suit		fruit		stew

Read the sentences and carefully trace the words.

Beth and Jed sit
still in the pew.

Adventures in Phonics - Level A

Remember to look at the vowels. Words on this page have the long sound of **u**.

rule

chew

drew

stew

screw

tune

new

pew

tube

fuse

juice

cube

Circle the correct word which matches the picture.

club
gum
nut

run
pup
hump

mug
gum
run

This lesson teaches how to mark long vowel words. Remember to think that the first vowel says its name, and the second vowel is silent.
On the list, mark the vowels in the word and then print the word under the correct picture. Repeat this process until you have used all the words in the list.

mūle	sūit	new (ū)

drew

flute

fruit

glue

mule

pew

rule

screw

stew

suit

tube

tune

Will you carefully print the words under the correct picture? Do you see that your printing is getting nicer? I think you are learning many important lessons.

Luke has a new blue suit.

flute cube chew juice				
tune glue fuse stew				
screw mule fruit pew				

Long Vowel - u - Words

u_e	**ew**	**ui**	**u_e** (yu)
t _ n _	f _ _	fr _ _ t	m _ l _
L _ k _	n _ _	s _ _ t	p _ r _
t _ b _	d _ _	j _ _ ce	c _ t _
fl _ t _	fl _ _	cr _ _ se	f _ m _

Add an **e** to make a long vowel sound word. Can you read all the words?

cut _____	tub _____	cub _____
us _____	can _____	rid _____
hat _____	pin _____	past _____

Complete these sentences with the missing words found in the box.

Luke	mule	fruit	cute	suit	blew

1. I can see a black _____.

2. It likes to eat _____.

3. The mule will go to _____.

4. Luke has on a _____ so he will not ride the mule.

5. The wind _____ a leaf on top of the mule.

6. The mule is _____.

This page is a review of the long **i**, **o** and **u**. Will you carefully print the words under the correct pictures? Remember: the first vowel says its name and the second vowel is silent.

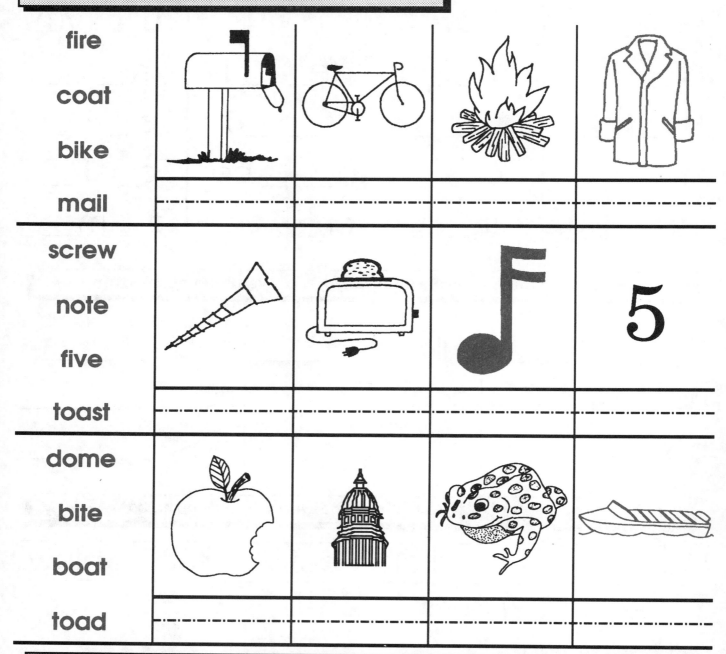

fire

coat

bike

mail

screw

note

five

toast

dome

bite

boat

toad

Read the sentences and carefully trace the words.

Mike rode a bike five miles.

Cones are fun to eat.

Review of Long Vowel Words

This is the first long vowel review sheet. Remember to think that the first vowel says its name, and the second vowel is silent. On the list, mark the vowels in the word and print the word under the picture. Repeat this process until you have used all the words in the list.

cāke

ear

fly

fruit

line

queen

slide

rake

stove

tree

vine

wheel

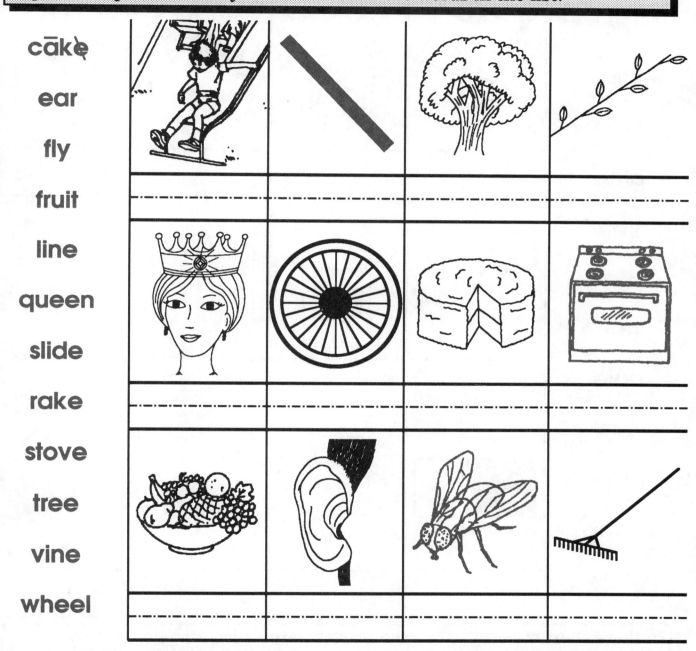

Read the sentence and carefully trace the words.

Is it time to go to the bank?

This is the second long vowel review sheet. On the list, mark the vowels in the word and print the word under the picture. Repeat this process until you have used all the words in the list.

coal
fuse
gate
glue
key
leaf
nail
pole
rain
rope
sheep
white

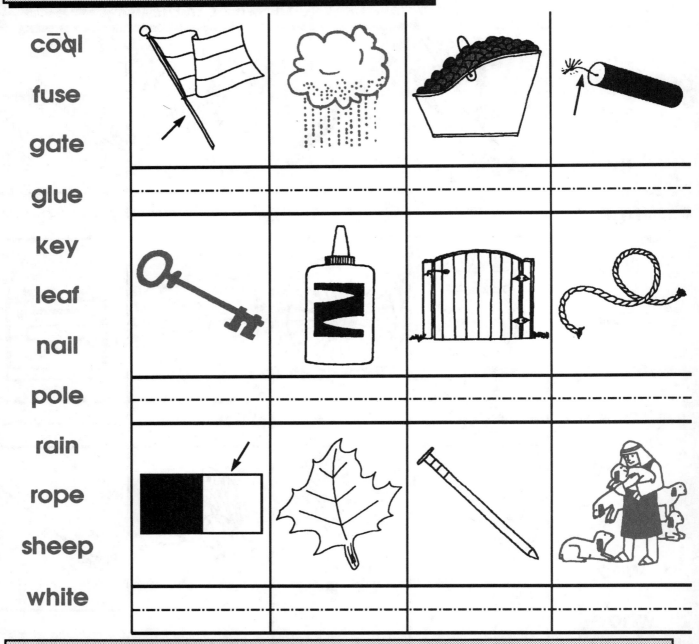

In these short **a** words, circle the correct word which matches the picture.

ant
wax
ax

yak
map
lamp

cat
lamp
bat

Review of Long Vowel Words

This is the third long vowel review sheet. On the list, mark the vowels in the word and print the word under the picture. Repeat this process until you have used all the words in the list.

bōwl

deer

hive

kite

lake

nose

note

pew

rose

sail

seat

wheat

In these short **u** words, circle the correct word which matches the picture.

cup
duck
plug

bug
drum
cuff

duck
plug
bug

This is the fourth long vowel review sheet. On the list, mark the vowels in the word and print the word under the picture. Repeat this process until you have used all the words in the list.

dīmȩ

dome

game

goat

heel

nine

pane

peas

pray

screw

seal

stew

In these short e words, circle the correct word which matches the picture.

pen
tent
bed

ten
egg
hen

bell
net
leg

Review of Long Vowel Words

This is the fifth long vowel review sheet. On the list, mark the vowels in the word and print the word under the picture. Repeat this process until you have used all the words in the list.

bēạds

bite

bone

dive

hay

new

snow

spray

teeth

toe

tube

yoke

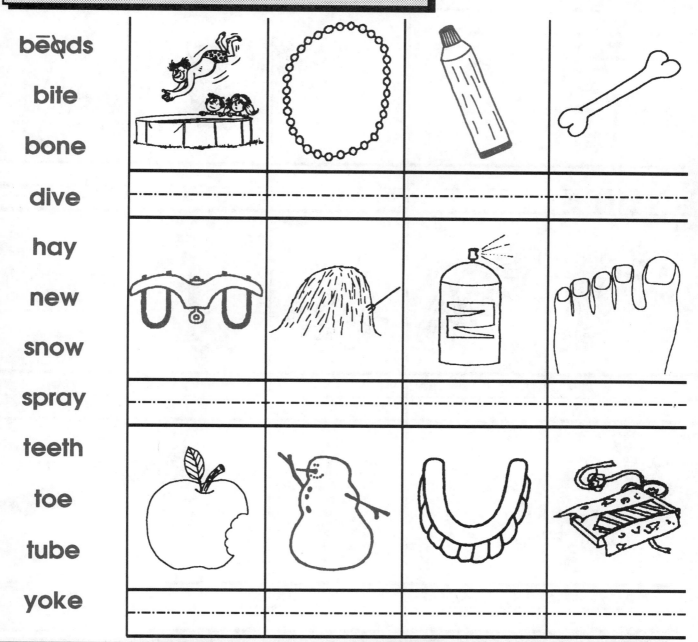

In these short **o** words, circle the correct word which matches the picture.

cot
doll
box

pop
sock
top

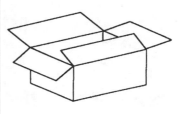

log
hop
box

Adventures in Phonics - Level A

Look in the boxes to see what vowels should be in the words below.

a_e	ee	i_e	o_e	u_e

vane

Do you still remember how to spell the short i words?

list
bib
fish

dish
six
sit

pig
hip
slip

Spelling Long Vowel Words

Look in the boxes to see what vowels should be
in the words below.

ai	oa	ui	ay	ea

bait

Do you still remember how to spell the short i words?

swim
trip
mitt

gum
sing
swim

bell
fell
wig

Adventures in Phonics - Level A

Look in the boxes to see what vowels should be in the words below.

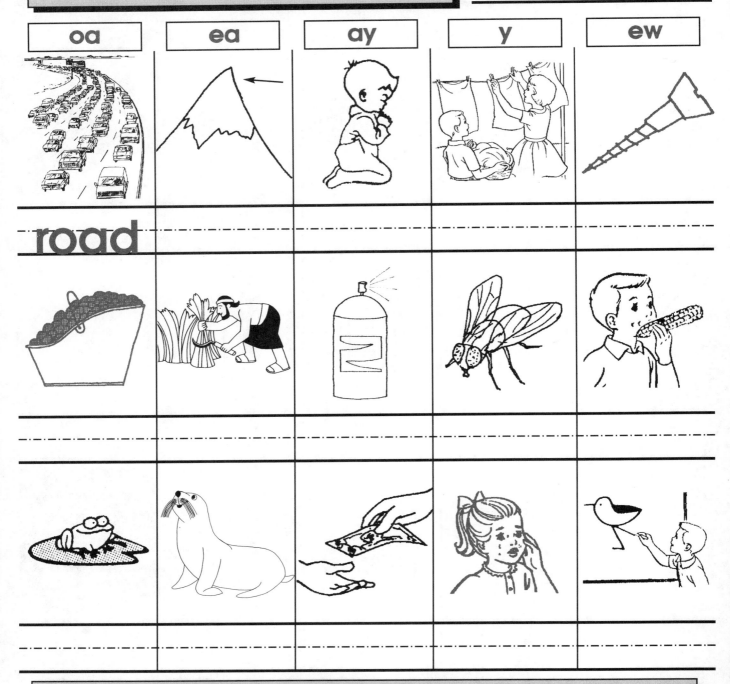

oa	ea	ay	y	ew

road

Do you still remember how to spell the long **ow** words?

bowl
crow
bow

snow
mow
flow

bowl
bow
crow

Long Vowel Sounds with Single - i - and - o -

> Usually the vowel **i** is short when it is alone in a word. This lesson teaches that the **i** is <u>long</u> when it is followed by **ld**, **nd** or **gh**. The **gh** is silent.

light

grind

right

fight

child

night

flight

kind

hind

fright

bind

bright

> Say each of these words three times as you trace over them.

light   sight   tight   fight   kind

find   mind   wild   mild   right

Adventures in Phonics - Level A

This lesson teaches that the **o** may have the long sound when it is followed by **ld, st, th, ll** or **lt**.

cold

post

roll

colt ------------------

bolt

stroll

fold

hold ------------------

Do you remember how to read these blend words? Underline the blends and print them where they belong.

prize

plug

plant

snail ------------------

Try to read these words. Will you read them three times?

old   sold   told   both   toll   bold   gold   host   most

Words with ow and ou Sounds

These words have two vowels that make a special sound that you may say when you get hurt. Two sets of vowels can make this sound, the **ow** as in cow and the **ou** as in house.

count				
crown	1 2 3 4 5 6 7 8 9			
mouth				
blouse	- - - - - - - - - -			
hound				
vowels		a e i o u	↓	
down				
scout	- - - - - - - - - -			

Draw a line from the word to the correct picture.

owl

round

mouse

clown

house

cow

Do you remember the sound that ou and ow make in these words?

house

cow

hour

clouds

snout

scout

mouse

pound

Need to buy:
*milk
*cereal
*coffee
*fruit
*meat

How do you spell these short i words?

Read the sentence and carefully trace the words.

God made the mountains.

Words with ow and ou Sounds

On this review page of the **ou** sound, underline the **ou** or the **ow** that makes that sound and carefully print the word. Repeat this process until you have used all the words in the list.

clouds

clown

count

cow

down

flower

mouth

owl

pound

round

thousand

vowels

1000

123456789

a e i o u

Circle the correct spelling of these **ay** words.

pray
hay
pay

tray
play
spray

pay
pray
tray

The consonant **r** has a strong sound. When it comes after a vowel, it changes or modifies that vowel sound. Mark the **a** like this: **ä**. Print the word under the correct picture.

ärk

barn

cart

Mark

dart

arch

march

car

Draw a line from the word to the correct picture.

harp

card

arm

jar

yarn

star

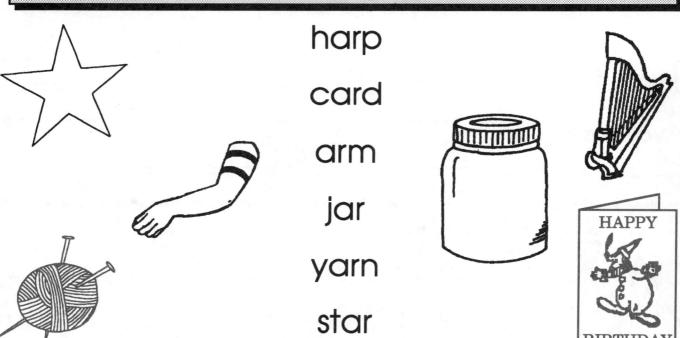

Words with är Sound

Do you remember the sound that **är** makes in these words?

harp

march

barn

alarm

farm

dart

car

ark

Try to complete these sentences from the words in the box.

barn	car	harp	yard	dart	ark

1. The cows are in the _____.

2. The law was kept in the _____.

3. Carl threw a _____.

4. Mark is to mow the front _____.

5. Dad drives a red _____.

6. Barb plays a _____ in church.

Do you remember the sound that **är** makes in these words?

dark

jar

shark

arch

Do you still remember how to print these **ou** and **ow** words?

hound

scout

vowels

mouse

a e i o u

Carefully trace and read these words.

shark dark bark spark park

alarm charm farm harm arm

dart art part start smart

star car bar tar par

Words with ôr and or Sounds

This lesson is about the modified vowel sound **or** as in corn. It is similar to the sound of the long **o**. The **o** may be marked like this **ô** or like this **ō**.

uniform				
core				
thorn				
stork				
organ				
storm		40		
forty				
corn				

Draw a line from the word to the correct picture.

door

horse

torch

fork

cord

horn

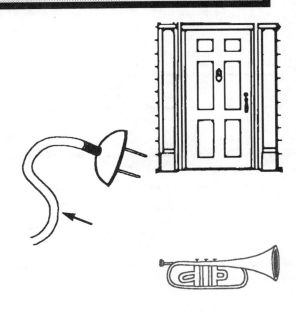

Remember the **ôr** sound as in corn. Underline the **ôr** sound in each word and carefully print it under the correct picture.

store

shore

snore

porch

acorn

thorn

cord

torn

Carefully trace and practice reading these words until you know them.

fork   torn   core   store

cork   born   pore   tore

pork   worn   sore   more

stork   Florida   score   snore

Words with ôr and or Sounds

Try to be very careful as you print these **or** words. Mark the **ôr** and print the words under the correct picture.

torch

core

corn

corner

fork

forty

horn

horse

shore

storm

stork

uniform

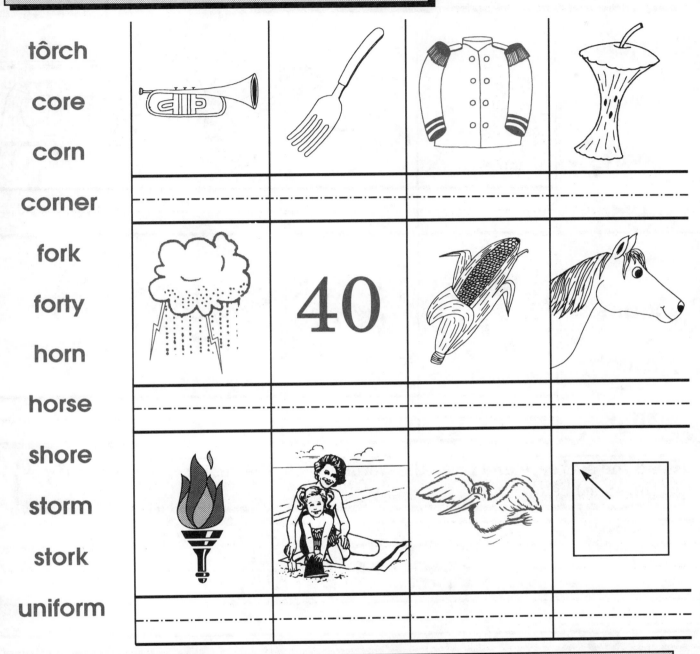

Do you remember how to spell these **a_e** words?

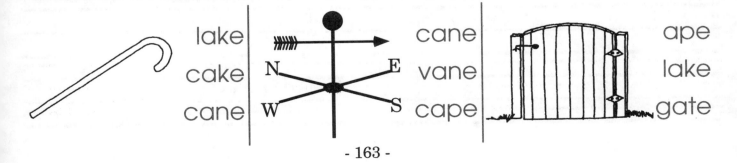

lake

cake

cane

cane

vane

cape

ape

lake

gate

Watch very carefully to see if the word has **ar** or **or**. Mark the **ôr** and **ăr** vowels and print the words in the proper places.

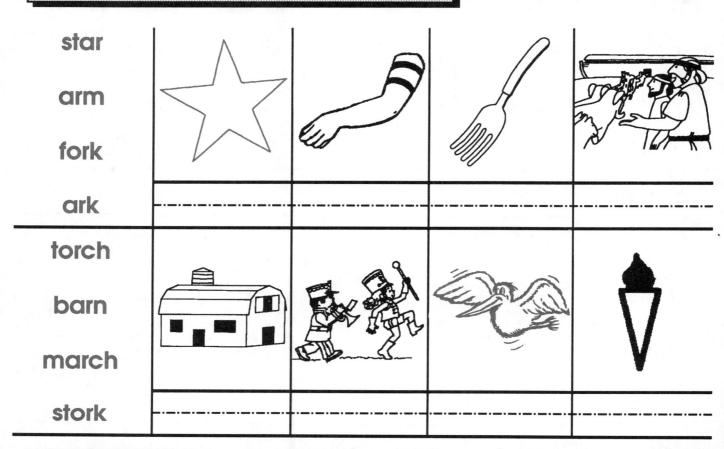

star

arm

fork

ark

torch

barn

march

stork

Read the sentence and trace the words. Write the sentence two more times in the space below.

The farmer plows his garden.

Words with ōō sound

The oo says the long u vowel sound in these words. Circle the correct word for each picture and write it in the space below.

goose cook loose	food tooth mood	spool fool tool	goose rooster roof
hoot boot toot	moose goose boot	scoot doom balloon	roof boot hoof
stoop troop spoon	tools fool zoom	booth food igloo	roof scoop zoom
zoo moo stool	broom brood mood	pool tool shoot	groom spoon snooze

Do you remember the sound of oo as in zoo?

moon

spoon

roof

rooster

kangaroo

spool

snooze

moose

Print these i_e words carefully under the pictures.

Words with o͞o sound

It is time to mark the **oo** in these words. After you have marked the sound like this **o͞o**, carefully print the word under the correct picture.

balloͦn

boot

broom

goose

moon

moose

raccoon

roof

rooster

snooze

spool

stool

Read the sentences and carefully trace the words.

Miss Roos sat on a stool.

She ate food with a spoon.

- 167 -

This lesson teaches that **oo** may also have the sound that is heard in book. Draw a line from the word to the correct picture.

book

cook

foot

hook

wood

shook

Try to complete these sentences from the words in the box.

cookies	hood	book	hook

1. Mother made good _____.

2. My coat has a _____.

3. When I go fishing I use a _____.

4. I like to read a _____.

Do you remember how to spell these oo words?

tooth

spool

food

moon

stool

boot

broom

food

boot

Words with oo Sound

Remember the sound of **oo** that you hear in book? That sound is also made by a **u** as in pull and **o** as in wolf. Read these words as you trace them.

put   wolves   wolf

pull   full   bush   push

Write the correct word under each picture.

cookies

push

wood

hook

_ _ _ _ _ _ _

book

pull

bush

hood

_ _ _ _ _ _ _

Another important way to spell the **oo** sound is with **ou**. Trace these words.

would   could   should

would   could   should

This is a review of the important sound **oo** (**u**). Do you remember all the ways to spell the **u** sound? Fill in the missing letters to discover the different ways the **u** sound is spelled.

scr**ew**	m**u**l**e**	fr**ui**t	gl**ue**	z**oo**
dr _ _	t _ b _	s _ _ t	bl _ _	g _ _ se
n _ _	c _ b _	j _ _ ce	cl _ _	t _ _ th
st _ _	c _ t _	cr _ _ se	fl _ _	m _ _ se
bl _ _	f _ s _	br _ _ se	S _ _	b _ _ th
fl _ _	fl _ t _	sl _ _ ce	h _ _	l _ _ se

The other sound of **oo** is **u**. Match the words with the pictures to find the other ways the **oo** sound can be spelled.

book
wolf
pull

book
wolf
pull

book
wolf
pull

Write the correct word under each picture.

foot

tube

stew

suit

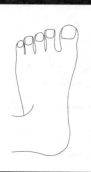

Words with oi and oy Sounds

A diphthong is a sound made up of two vowels blended together to make one sound. This lesson teaches the sound of the diphthongs **oi** and **oy**.

boy

foil

point

soil

noise

coins

toy

oil

cowboy

coil

voice

poison

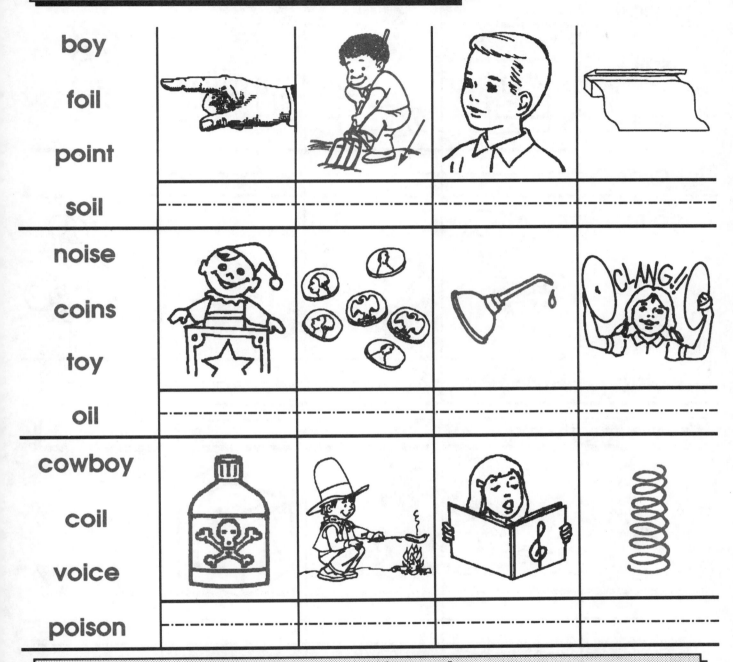

Read the sentences and carefully trace the words.

Joy gave Roy a new toy cowboy.

Wag makes a loud noise.

Remember the diphthong sound of **oi** and **oy**.
Underline the **oi** or **oy** and print the word.

p<u>oi</u>son

soil

coil

noise

coins

oil

toy

point

Can you print these **ck** words?

Read the sentence and carefully trace the letters.

Ray may play with clay today.

Words with oi and oy Sounds

Print **oi** in the middle of the words, and **oy** when that sound comes at the end of the words.

v__ce   b__l   b__   t__l

n__se   j__n   f__l   m__st

j__   br__l   c__l   R__

j__nt   t__   p__nt   h__st

How do you spell these **y** words? Write the correct word under each picture.

dry

sky

fly

cry

How do you spell these **sh** words? Write the correct word under each picture.

shell

dish

ship

brush

You have studied about **ar** as in car and **or** as in corn. The other three vowels are also modified, or changed, by the letter **r**.

When **e**, **i** and **u** are followed by an **r**, they make the same sound. They sound just like a rooster when it crows.

er   ir   ur

church			
bird			
purse		If you confess with your mouth Jesus as Lord, and believe in your heart that God raised Him from the dead, you shall be saved. Romans 10:9	
verse			
turtle			
thirty		30	
giraffe			
water			
turkey			
zipper			
nurse			
skirt			

Words with er, ir, ur, ear and (w)or

squirrel

cracker

shirt

girl

hammer

fern

rocker

mother

Carefully trace and read these **er**, **ir** and **ur** words.

curl burn turn hurt fur

girl first third dirt stir

Do these words have **or** or **ar**? Spell each word.

You have learned that **er**, **ir** and **ur** say the same sound. Two more ways to spell the **er** sound are **ear** as in earth and **(w)or** as in world.

ear
as in earth

(w)or
as in world

Underline the letters that say the **er** sound and print the words.

w<u>o</u>rm

fern

nurse

shirt

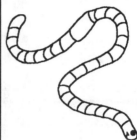

Do you remember how to spell these **ng** and **nk** words?

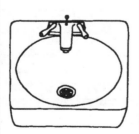

Read and carefully trace these words.

learn   earn   heard   early   words

Words with er, ir, ur, ear and (w)or

Practice reading these words. Print them at the end of the correct sentence.

verse	shirt	world	learn	bird	church	Word

1. Bill went with his father and mother to _____.

2. He put on his new _____.

3. He could say his Bible _____.

4. He will learn that God made this big _____.

5. The Bible is God's _____.

6. The Bible has much for us to _____.

7. Bill heard the chirp of a _____.

Underline the letters that say the er sound and print the words.

church				
pitcher	13			
rocker				
thirteen	- - - - -	- - - - -	- - - - -	- - - - -
turkey				
world				
worm				
zipper	- - - - -	- - - - -	- - - - -	- - - - -

Past lessons have taught other sounds of the vowel o: short o as in ox; long o as in oak; oo as in spoon; and oo as in book. This page teaches another sound which the o may make: ô as in dog. Underline the o sound in each of these words and print them under the correct picture.

log

cloth

frog

moth

cross

dog

off

hog

Learn these words as you trace and read them.

cost frost long soft hog

Think about the vowel sound of the o in each word.

Words with the Sound of - ô -

Remember the sound of **ô** as in dog. The vowel **a** makes this same sound when it is followed by an **l**, **w** or **u**. For example, **al** as in call, **aw** as in saw and **ua** as in haul.

claw

ball

draw

saw

hawk

jaw

salt

paw

Print these words and sentences as you carefully read them out loud.

tawn   fault   halt   chalk   halt

dawn   flaw   malt   tall   small

Jesus died on the cross for us.

I am so glad I belong to Him.

You have learned that the ô sound may be made by these letters: **o** as in dog; **al** as in call; **au** as in haul; **aw** as in saw. This lesson teaches that **augh** and **ough** make that sound also. The **gh** letters are silent.

caught				
daughter				
naughty				
taught				

It is time to review other words which have the ô sound. Underline the ô sound in each of these words and print them under the correct picture.

p<u>aw</u>				
law				
salt				
frog				
awning				
cloth				
straw				
fall				

Words with the Sound of - ô -

As you do this review page, remember the many ways the **ô** sound may be spelled.

ô	**al**	**au**	**aw**	**ough**	**augh**
dog	call	haul	saw	fought	caught

Underline the letters that say the **ô** sound and print the words.

awning

ball

claw

cross

daughter

hawk

hog

jaw

law

moth

off

salt

Read the sentence and carefully trace the words.

Paul will haul the laundry.

Adventures in Phonics - Level A

This is review sheet number one. Say the words and each of the sounds below.

är arm | ôr ōr corn | ou ow cow | oi oy boy | o͝o o͞o book moon | ô al aw au ough augh aw saw | er ur (w)or ir ear skirt

Underline the sounds in each word and print the words under the pictures.

blouse
boot
broom
car
cross
dart
hook
point
purse
soil
vowels
yarn

a e i o u

Review of Words with Sounds

är arm	**ôr** **ōr** corn	**ou** **ow** cow	**oi** **oy** boy	**ŏŏ** **ōō** book moon	**ô al aw au** **ough augh** **aw** saw	**er ur ear** **(w)or** **ir** skirt

Underline the sounds in each word and print the words under the pictures.

<u>aw</u>ning

card

football

hot dog

north

nurse

oil

skirt

star

thorn

thousand

zipper

1000

- 183 -

Adventures in Phonics - Level A

This is review sheet number three. Say the words and each of the sounds below.

är arm **ôr ōr** corn **ou ow** cow **oi oy** boy **o͝o o͞o** book moon **ô al aw au ough augh aw** saw **er ur (w)or ir** skirt

Underline the sounds in each word and print the words under the pictures.

bush
cook
jar
moose
mountain
paw
poison
shirt
spool
store
wood
world

Review of Words with Sounds

This is review sheet number four. Say the words and each of the sounds below.

är arm	ôr / ōr corn	ou / ow cow	oi / oy boy	ŏŏ / ōō book moon	ô al aw au ough augh aw saw	er ur ear (w)or ir skirt

Underline the sounds in each word and print the words under the pictures.

<u>ar</u>ch

clouds

down

fern

harp

meal

rooster

salt

scout

strong

turkey

turtle

- 185 -

Adventures in Phonics - Level A

är arm	ôr / ōr corn	ou ow cow	oi oy boy	ŏŏ book / ōō moon	ô al aw au ough augh aw saw	er ur ear (w)or ir skirt

Underline the sounds in each word and print the words under the pictures.

ark

caught

church

cloth

cookies

core

crown

foil

naughty

push

spoon

worm

Review of Words with Sounds

Look in the boxes to see what vowels should be in the words below. Try to spell the words.

Look in the boxes to see what vowels should be in the words below. Try to spell the words.

all	oi	ou	(w)or	ô
			er Children, obey your parents in the Lord for this is right. Ephesians 6:1	
	oy		**er**	ON
	oy		**ear**	

Review of Words with Sounds

Look in the boxes to see what vowels should be in the words below. Try to spell the words.

aw	ur	or	o͝o	oi

You have learned that **ăr** is in arm. The **ar** may also sound like **âr** as in square. The **âr** sound may be made by the following letters:

are square	**arr** carrot	**air** chair	**err** berry	**ear** bear	**ere** where

Underline the sounds in each word and print the words under the pictures.

b<u>ear</u>

berry

carrot

carry

chair

cherry

hair

pear

square

stairs

tear

where

Words with âr Sound

You have learned that **är** is in arm. The **ar** may also sound like **âr** as in square. The **âr** sound may be made by the following letters:

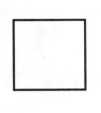 **are** square |  **arr** carrot |  **air** chair |  **err** berry |  **ear** bear |  **ere** where

Read the sentence and draw a line from the sentence to the picture.

Where is the carrot?   There is the chair.

Where is the square?   There is the pear.

Where is the pear?      There is the berry.

Where is the chair?   There is the carrot.

Where is the berry?   There is the square.

Do you still remember how to read and circle the correct word?

wall
fall
ball

joint
coins
point

map
law
march

towel
crow
hook

(globe)
earth
chair
book

saw
off
cough

You have learned that **är** is in arm. The **ar** may also sound like **âr** as in square. The **âr** sound may be made by the following letters:

are square	**arr** carrot	**air** chair	**err** berry	**ear** bear	**ere** where

Underline the letters that make the **âr** sound and print the words.

b<u>ear</u>

carry

hair

chariot

Do you remember how to read and print these words?

40

Read the sentences and carefully trace these words.

The law of the Lord is perfect.

The earth is the Lord's.

Words with âr Sound

ēar	⇨	tear	dear	gear	hear

ear	⇨	earth	learn	heard	earn

eâr	⇨	tear	pear	bear	wear

Underline the letters that say the **âr** sound and print the words.

bear

berry

chair

chariot

hair

pear

stairs

tear

Read the sentence and carefully trace these words.

We should care about others.

This lesson teaches a very important fact about the consonant **c**. It makes the hard sound of **k** when the vowels **a**, **o** and **u** come after the **c**. Examples are cat, cot and cut. The consonant **c** usually makes the soft sound as in **s** when **e**, **i** or **y** come after the letter.

ice   city   cymbals

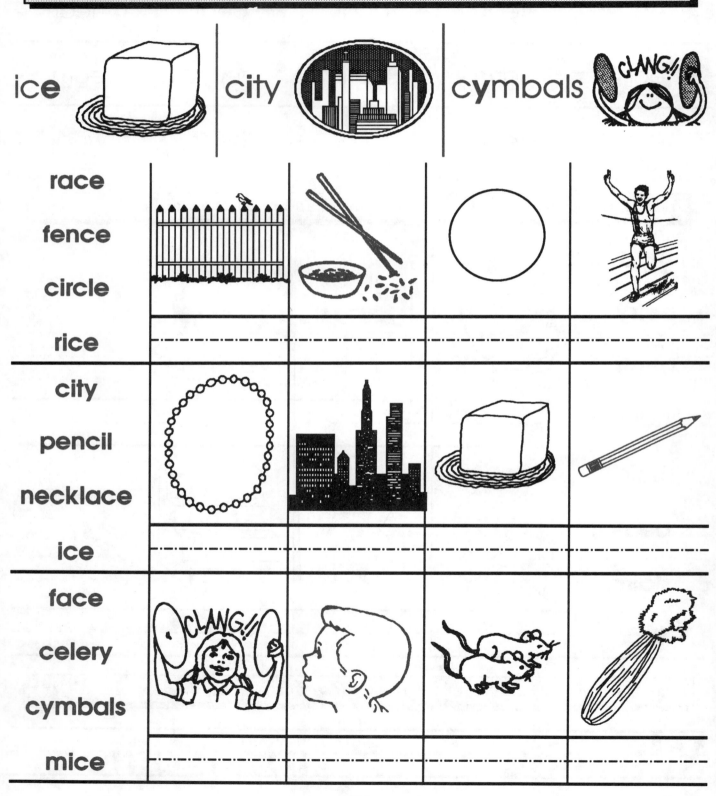

race			
fence			
circle			
rice			
city			
pencil			
necklace			
ice			
face			
celery			
cymbals			
mice			

Review of the Long and Short Sound of - a -

Do you remember the long and short sounds of **a**? Print the name under each of these pictures.

a_e	a_e	ai	ai	ay
take				

Circle the correct name which matches the picture.

tag
bag
slack

van
can
rat

jam
jar
fan

Just as the **c** makes the sound of **s** when **e**, **i** or **y** comes after it, the **g** usually makes a soft sound of **j** when **e**, **i** or **y** follows it. For example, cage, gym and giant. Underline the **e**, **i** or **y** that makes the **g** have the soft sound of **j**. Read these words three times before you print them in the spaces.

badge

bridge

engine

gem

giraffe

hinge

large

pledge

From the list of words above, read and complete the sentences.

1. Bruce has a big train _____.

2. At the zoo we saw a large _____.

3. Dad drove our car on a _____.

4. The door has a black _____.

5. All policemen must wear a _____.

6. Do not forget to say the _____.

7. A diamond is a very nice _____.

Do you remember the long and short sounds of **i**? The words in this first part are spelled **i_e**.

These words make the **g** have the sound of **j**.

bridge

giraffe

engine

hinge

Circle the correct long vowel **y** word which matches each picture.

cry	sky	cry
dry	shy	dry
fly	fry	sky

Adventures in Phonics - Level A

Do you remember the digraphs **sh**, **ch**, **wh** and **th**? Say their sounds three times. Now you will learn two more digraphs: **kn** as in knot and **wr** as in write. The **k** is silent when followed by **n**. The **w** is silent when followed by **r**. Draw a line through the **k** or **w** and read the words three times before you print.

knee

kneel

knife

knock

knot

knuckle

wren

wrench

wring

wrinkle

write

wrong

$$\begin{array}{ccc} 4 & 2 & 3 \\ +2 & +5 & +2 \\ \hline 6 & 7 & 4\checkmark \end{array}$$

Read the sentence and carefully trace the words.

I know I went the wrong way.

The Letters ing and Review of kn and wr

You may remember that **ing** is in these words. Listen for this sound as you carefully print the words.

The **ing** may also be added to the end of the <u>root</u> or main word. Then the **ing** is called a <u>suffix</u>. Print these words and add the suffix **ing**.

pick _picking_   talk _____   sing _____
jump _____   walk _____   ring _____
tell _____   see _____   pray _____
help _____   cook _____   add _____
puff _____   go _____   fly _____
look _____   roll _____   cry _____

Just as the **k** is silent when followed by **n** in the digraph **kn**, the **g** is silent when followed by **n** in the digraph **gn** as in gnat.

gnat

kneel

knife

write

You have learned that the **y** is a vowel when it is at the end of a word. When the **y** is the only vowel in the word, it has the long **i** sound as in fly. When the **y** follows another vowel, the **y** is usually silent as in day or key. When the word has other vowels somewhere in the word, the **y** has the long sound of **e** as in baby. Read these words three times and print them in the correct columns.

by	my	windy	why	cry
happy	funny	fly	needy	Mary
shy	try	dry	weary	fry
silly	rocky	hilly	sky	penny

y has long i sound | | **y has long e sound** |

by		happy	

You know that the vowels **ea** make the long sound of **e** as in bean. Sometimes the **ea** may have the short sound of **e** as in head. Mark the **e** short in these words as you read and print them.

brĕad

feather

sweater

head

Adding Suffixes er, y and ing

Do you remember what the important word called the suffix means? It is an ending added to a main word or root word. The suffix helps us to use root words in many ways. You have learned the **ing** suffix. The **er** is also a suffix. Draw a line from the root word in the sentence to the new word with the suffix added.

1. If you help you are a   talker
2. If you talk you are a   jumper
3. If you jump you are a   helper
4. If you work you are a   fusser
5. If you fuss you are a   eater
6. If you eat you are an   worker

7. If you climb you are a   sleeper
8. If you sleep you are a   thinker
9. If you play you are a   singer
10. If you sing you are a   player
11. If you walk you are a   climber
12. If you think you are a   walker

Add **ing** to these words and draw a line to match them with the pictures.

read <u>i n g</u>

jump _____

knock _____

pick _____

pray _____

bowl _____

The next suffix is a **y**. When **y** is at the end of a word, it is a vowel. If it is the only vowel in the word, it has the long vowel sound of **i** as in fly. But in these words it says the long sound of **e**. Make new words by adding **y**.

dust _____	hill _____	wind _____
crust _____	puff _____	bump _____
rock _____	fuzz _____	milk _____
sleep _____	rust _____	need _____
weed _____	lump _____	sand _____

You have learned how to read the word mother. Notice that the **o** makes the short vowel sound of **u**. In many other words the **o** also may have the short **u** sound. Read and trace the following words. Notice that some of the words end with an **e** because words never end with the letter **v**.

mother   other   brother

from   some   come   of

front   son   won   ton

dove   love   shove   glove

Each of the vowels may sometimes make the short sound of **u**. In a dictionary you may see a symbol like this **ə** which is called a schwa. It stands for the short **u** sound. In these words the beginning **a** has the schwa sound. Read the words and divide them as you print. Notice that the vowels in the second syllable or part of the words obey vowel rules you have already learned.

astray a-s-t-r-a-y	around _____	about _____
awake _____	afraid _____	arose _____
awhile _____	apart _____	alone _____
alike _____	away _____	ago _____
along _____	ahead _____	avoid _____
alive _____	aloud _____	asleep _____

Compound Words, Review of Schwa Sound and ea Sound

Sometimes two words may be written right next to each other to form a compound word. The two words in each space may be written together. Read them two times after you have written them.

with out	book case	side walk	rain bow
without			
wind mill	dust pan	cob web	sand box
rain drops	him self	tea spoon	bed room

Underline the letters that say the short e sound and print the words.

feather				
bread				
thread				
sweater				

Choose one of the words in the box to complete the sentence.

alike	about	arose	afraid	asleep

1. Our Lord _____ from the grave.
2. The twin brothers look _____.
3. God is with us so we will not be _____.
4. Mother read to us _____ a gray pup.
5. Dan fell _____ for he was very tired.

Adventures in Phonics - Level A

You have learned that some consonants are silent in digraphs such as **kn, gn** and **wr**. In a few other sets of letters, one consonant or vowel may also be silent, such as: **mb** as in limb, **bt** as in doubt, **gu** as in guess and **bu** as in build. Read these words several times as you write them under the correct picture.

climb

tomb

build

limb

Make new words by adding these suffixes.

	ing	er	ed	s
play				
help				
walk				
jump				

Where do these âr words belong? square, chariot, chair, bear, carry

- 204 -

Using an or a in Sentences

When one object is mentioned, the word <u>an</u> or <u>a</u> may be used when talking about the object. For example: <u>a car</u> or <u>an ark</u>. Notice that an <u>a</u> is used before a word that begins with a consonant, and the word <u>an</u> is used before a word that begins with a vowel. Put the correct word on the spaces below.

<u>a</u> wall   ___ bird   ___ ox   ___ man

<u>an</u> apple   ___ pen   ___ egg   ___ door

___ light   ___ ark   ___ ball   ___ home

___ ant   ___ inch   ___ toy   ___ box

___ elk   ___ tree   ___ ax   ___ clock

Do you remember the ô sound spelled with these letters? **augh -- caught, o -- dog, al -- call, au -- haul, aw -- saw, ough -- fought**

awning

hawk

daughter

fawn

law

moth

off

taught

You have learned that an **s** is added to most words when more than one object is mentioned. For example egg or eggs. More than one means plural. If a word ends with **y**, two rules need to be learned. The first rule is: <u>when the **y** follows a vowel, just add **s**.</u>

toy __ | day __ | boy __ | turkey __

joy __ | ray __ | way __ | valley __

play __ | key __ | tray __ | donkey __

The second rule is: <u>when the **y** follows a consonant, change the **y** to **i** and add **es**.</u> Have your teacher help you read these words three times. Do with each word as the example shows you.

lady <u>ladies</u> | city _____ | berry _____

baby _____ | sky _____ | bunny _____

copy _____ | cry _____ | party _____

pony _____ | fly _____ | penny _____

story _____ | lily _____ | puppy _____

Where do these words belong? arch, crown, fern, core, dart

Review of Silent Consonants

Think again about some consonants which are silent as in these words. Print the words in the correct spaces and cross out the silent consonant.

_____

_____

lamb̶	knife	gnat	hymn	knee
climb	wrong	knot	thumb	knock

$\begin{array}{ccc} 4 & 2 & 3 \\ +2 & +5 & +2 \\ \hline 6 & 7 & 4 \checkmark \end{array}$

Thomas O. Chisholm

1. "Great is thy faith - ful - ness," O
2. Sum - mer and win - ter, and sprir
3. Par - don for sin and a peac

Can you see the two words in these compound words? Divide the words by drawing a line between them.

rain\coat	beside	oatmeal	hayride
rowboat	beehive	pancake	sunset
necktie	into	seahorse	mailbox
baseball	cupcake	inside	himself

Do you remember the two rules that teach how to make words that end with **y** into plural words? They are listed in the box below. Look carefully at the letter that comes just before the **y**. Make these words mean more than one.

* Do not change the **y** when it is after a vowel.
* Change the **y** to **i** and add **es**, when the **y** comes after a consonant.

lady <u>ladies</u>	key _____	tray _____
baby _____	valley _____	party _____
toy _____	day _____	play _____
story _____	joy _____	turkey _____
pony _____	copy _____	boy _____

Print the word under the correct picture.

barn

dress

gift

mouse

rooster

stool

top

tub

Review of - o - Sound and Digraphs kn and wr

_____

_____

mother	son	month	love
brother	Monday	come	some

1. Tom will have his sixth birthday in the _____ of May.

2. His _____ will have a party for him next _____.

3. His family will _____ and bring him _____ presents.

4. They will come because they _____ Tom.

5. He has an older _____, so Tom is the youngest _____.

Think again about the sounds **kn** and **wr** make. Print the word under the correct picture.

kneel			
knife			
knock			
knot			
wring			
wrinkle			
write			
wrong			

Adventures in Phonics - Level A

> What happens when **e**, **i** or **y** come after a **c** or **g**?
> * The letter **c** usually has the sound of **s**.
> * The letter **g** usually has the sound of **j**.

pencil				
city				
race				
circle				
bridge				
hinge				
engine				
giraffe				
gem				
ice				
celery				
large				

> **Print the correct word in the blank to complete the sentence.**

giraffe	pledge	mice	rice	large	cage

1. Two little _____ came and ate our _____.

2. A _____ crowd said the _____ to the flag.

3. We saw a _____ in a large _____ at the zoo.

Review of the Doubled Consonants and the ck Sound

When a word has a **short vowel sound**, usually the consonants **s**, **f**, **l** and **z** will be doubled. You know many of these words already. Some exceptions are bus, gas, yes, as, is, has, was and his. Underline the double consonant and write the word under the correct picture.

cuff				
bell				
kiss				
hill				
glass				
dress				
quill				
doll				

Remember that **ck** is used at the end of short vowel words ending in a **k** sound. Choose the correct **ck** word in the box to complete the sentence.

black	rocks	quack	duck
back	trick	stick	crack

1. A _____ truck had a load of _____.

2. Mr. Nick did a _____ with a _____.

3. Jack's little pet _____ said _____.

4. Dick fell on his _____ as he tripped on a _____.

An **a** is used before a word beginning with a consonant: **a** car, **a** tree, **a** lamb. The word **an** is used before a word beginning with a vowel: **an** ark, **an** elephant, **an** ant. Print **a** or **an** correctly in these sentences.

1. Sam can see _____ bug and _____ ant on _____ log.

2. Mother will open _____ door and turn on _____ light.

3. Tom ate _____ egg and _____ muffin for breakfast.

4. Dad cut down _____ tree with _____ ax.

5. Bill hit _____ ball with _____ bat.

6. We saw _____ elk and _____ bear in the woods.

7. Have you ever seen _____ squirrel eat _____ apple?

Can you print these ô words?

Choose the correct word in the box to complete the sentence.

laws	taught	Talk	all	daughter

1. Mr. Hall read from the Bible to his _____.

2. We ought to obey _____ of God's _____.

3. Your teacher has _____ you many lessons.

4. _____ to your teacher about your thankfulness.

Trust in the Lord with all your heart,
And do not lean on your own understanding.
In all your ways acknowledge Him,
and He will make your paths straight.
Proverbs 3:5-6

Delight yourself in the Lord;
and He will give you the desires of your heart.
Commit your way to the Lord,
Trust also in Him, and He will do it.
And He will bring forth your righteousness
as the light,
And your judgment as the noonday.
Psalms 37:4-6

The Alphabet

Here is a chart to help you study how to properly write the letters and numbers.

Upper and Lower Case Letters

This chart will help you learn the differences between the upper and lower case letters.

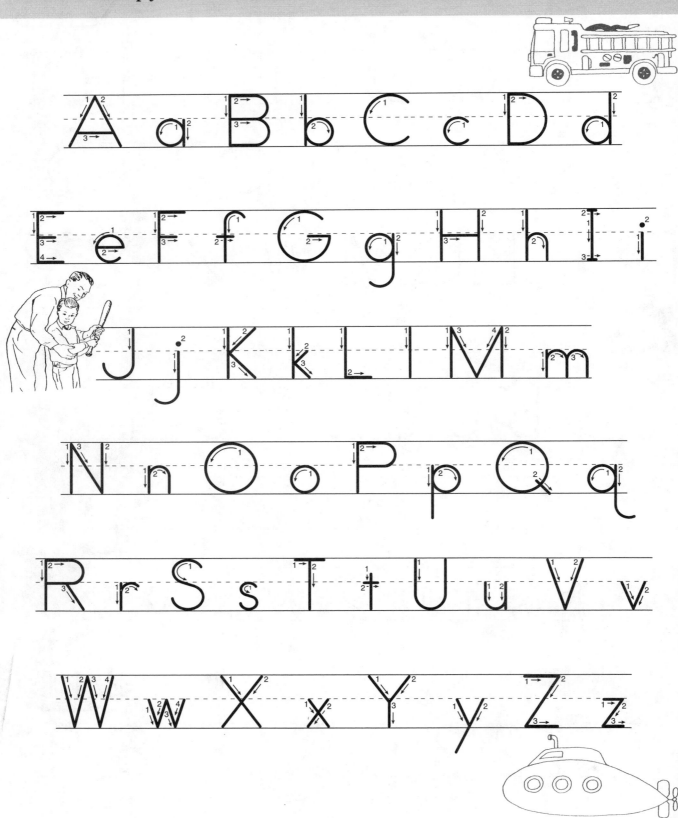